BEGIN'S ISRAEL,
MUBARAK'S EGYPT

BEGIN'S ISRAEL, MUBARAK'S EGYPT

Alex Chapman

W. H. Allen · London
A Howard & Wyndham Company
1983

Copyright © Alex Chapman 1983

Phototypeset by Input Typesetting Ltd, London
Printed and bound in Great Britain by
Mackays of Chatham Ltd, Kent
for the Publishers, W. H. Allen & Co. Ltd,
44 Hill Street, London W1X 8LB

ISBN 0 491 03381 8

All photographs, unless otherwise credited, courtesy of the Israel
Press Association.

Contents

To my mother

Preface

It is the aim of this book to further a greater understanding of the crises which perennially wrack the Middle East by setting out, in plain terms, the background to those events. At moments of crisis the press and the media lack the time to give enough in-depth information to make them fully comprehensible, let alone enable the viewer or reader to place them in their proper historical and political context. It is hoped that this book will go some way to fill such a gap. It is intended for the general reader, not for the specialist. It does not presume to suggest solutions to contemporary problems; rather it seeks to provide the reader with the tools to approach them with fresh insight and to enhance his understanding of future events as and when they occur.

Why write a book about Egypt and Israel? Firstly, because Israel is the undisputed catalyst of the region, while Egypt is the most powerful and populous Arab country. Secondly, because Israel has always been perceived by her neighbours as a hostile and predatory intruder, while Egypt has embodied Arab rejection of the Zionist state. It is the author's belief that presenting Egypt and Israel each through their own eyes casts new light on the totally different nature of their political and historical experience and the gulf that lies between their social and economic expectations. These are two radically diverse perceptions, and their relevance extends to the whole of the Middle East. Policy-makers neglect this dimension at their peril. In Europe and the United States plans for peace and stability in the region have repeatedly been formulated only to be confounded when decisive events in the area happen without external help or interference.

Shortly before he resigned, Menachem Begin was asked how he would like to be remembered. He replied: as the man who had set the borders of the land of Israel for all eternity. This reflects the essence of his political style. During the thirty years of Labour government, he single-mindedly advocated Jewish expansion over all the territory of the ancient land of Israel. His idea of compromise was reluctant acquiescence in the loss of the east bank of the Jordan. At the time of the Israeli withdrawal from Sinai in the wake of the peace treaty with Egypt, many observers reflected upon the seeming ease with which he felt able to withdraw from the new Israeli settlements which had cost millions of dollars to establish. In fact, he had no ideological objection to withdrawal from an area which had never been considered the land of Israel. He saw no contradiction at all between withdrawal from Sinai and annexation of East Jerusalem and the Golan Heights. One thing is sure: by his unswerving commitment to expanding Jewish settlement in the West Bank, Menachem Begin has permanently altered Israel's political consensus and certainly her ultimate borders.

Part I

BEGIN'S ISRAEL

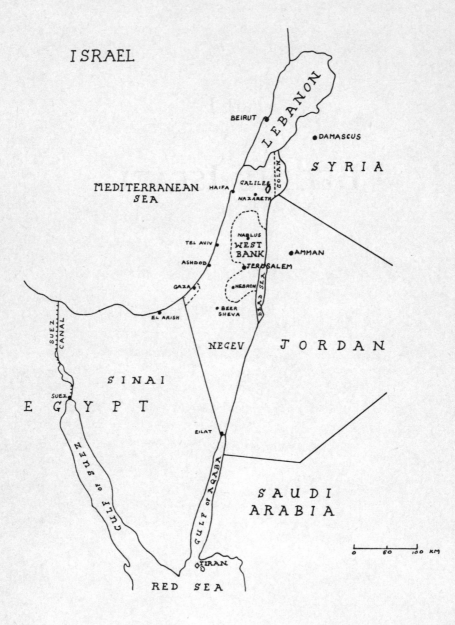

ISRAEL

LEBANON

BEIRUT

DAMASCUS

SYRIA

MEDITERRANEAN
SEA

HAIFA

GALILEE

GOLAN

NAZARETH

TEL AVIV

NABLUS

WEST
BANK

AMMAN

ASHDOD

JERUSALEM

GAZA

HEBRON

DEAD SEA

EL ARISH

BEER
SHEVA

NEGEV

JORDAN

SUEZ CANAL

SINAI

SUEZ

EGYPT

GULF OF SUEZ

EILAT

SAUDI
ARABIA

GULF OF AQABA

0   50   100 KM

TIRAN

RED SEA

1

Before the Birth of the State

Israel came into being from a mixture of lofty idealism and dire necessity. When, in 1882, Rothschild purchased his initial plots of land from Turkish absentee landlords and assisted the first wave of settlers, he was giving expression to the potent, mystical Zionist pledge that one day the diaspora would end and the Jews return to a land that was theirs. The social idealism of most of the first and second generation of settlers, pent up during one thousand years of living in alien societies, was also a powerful motive force. Only in the 1930s and '40s, when the predicament of Jews in much of Europe deteriorated beyond their worst expectations, did the Zionist movement launch a desperate rescue operation. Today new generations of settlers and internal demographic change have created fresh forces in Israeli society. More than half the population are not Jews of Western origin; religious groups are more strident; the Arabs are still not reconciled; and wars recur with discouraging regularity. Some of the Western Jews feel that their ideals are threatened and undervalued. They are confused by the criticism levelled at Israel by the world at large, and being by nature self-analytical they have become uneasy about what is happening in their society. This opening chapter will briefly examine the roots of that society and of the state; for many of the attitudes and apparent contradictions in Israel today stem from those roots.

13

The motive force which kept the dream alive, and indeed preserved the Jewish identity, was religion. It was scattered, fervently religious communities who kept the Jewish presence alive in the Holy Land through the centuries of the diaspora in the four Holy Cities: Jerusalem, Sfat, Hebron and Tiberius. It was through the synagogues in the diaspora that money was channelled to support these communities, and later to sponsor the Zionist Movement. The little Haluka collecting-box stood on every mantelpiece.

The Zionist Movement gathered strength in the second half of the nineteenth century, at first in Russia, where the pressure of pogroms was greatest, and then in other European centres. Zionists believed in the desirability of a return of the Jews to their homeland, Palestine. The idea had been aired both in Jewish and Christian circles for at least two hundred years before the movement reached take-off point in 1896 with the publication of Theodor Herzl's book, *The Jewish State*. From 1889 onwards there were regular World Zionist Congresses. Rothschild's private philanthropy could never bring about a Jewish state, nor could Herzl's book, but both helped to persuade some politicians in Europe to take the idea seriously. If Herzl conceived the project, the midwife was Chaim Weizmann; a distinguished immigrant chemist at Manchester University and an inspired public relations expert.

Weizmann was a compelling personality with considerable charm, and he went to work on the British political scene; for both Herzl and Weizmann were agreed that Britain was the country in the best position to sponsor their aspirations. Since 1839 Britain had had a special relationship with the Jews in Palestine, in that she had undertaken to protect the interests of Jews living there under Turkish rule. Weizmann exercised his charisma on any members of the establishment he could reach through his key contact, Lord Simon. He did not talk about a new state, but simply of a 'British protectorate over a Jewish homeland', which reduced his

14

demand to the scale of routine land concessions familiar to the British at that time in the context of Rhodesia or East Africa. One has to bear in mind that this was at the height of the British colonialist era. At one point the Zionists were actually offered a part of the East African Highlands for their purpose; but Weizmann knew his fellow Zionists, and perhaps his Christian sponsors as well, and held out for the Holy Land. Balfour said, later: 'It was from Weizmann that I saw that the Jewish form of patriotism was unique. Their love of country refused to be satisfied by the Uganda scheme. It was Weizmann's absolute refusal even to look at it that impressed me.' The romantic sense of historical destiny that was kindled by the idea of the Return in the hearts of non-Jewish statesmen, from Winston Churchill to Lloyd George and Balfour, is a phenomenon not easy to understand today. In any case it only explains the background climate to the more hard-headed political considerations.

In 1914, at the beginning of the war, Lloyd George had proposed simply annexing the Holy Land. In his eyes British rule over a Jewish Palestine would have represented a logical *tour de force* of international diplomacy. In 1917, Allenby and the British forces in Egypt drove out the Turks and occupied Palestine, so Britain was in a position to back up vague propositions with action. Lloyd George, then Prime Minister, was persuaded that a grateful American Jewish lobby would nudge the United States into the war, while Foreign Secretary Balfour and other members of the Cabinet were convinced that a body of European, albeit Jewish, settlers would help to stabilise the Near East and protect the northern frontier of Egypt and the approaches to the Suez Canal. So the historic letter to Rothschild was drafted and signed with full Cabinet approval on 29 May 1917, containing what is known as the Balfour Declaration:

15

'His Majesty's Government view with favour the establishment in Palestine of a national home for the Jewish people, and will use their best endeavours to facilitate the achievement of this object, it being clearly understood that nothing shall be done to prejudice the civil and religious rights of existing non-Jewish communities in Palestine, or the rights and political status enjoyed by Jews in any other country.'

And there stand some of the historic phrases that have bedevilled the politics of the area ever since. Did the establishment of a national home in Palestine mean Palestine was to be the national home of the Jews? Evidently not, for only four years after the Declaration Britain amputated about one third of the area, that part to the east of the river Jordan, and set up one of her protégés, the Hashemite Emir Abdullah, in a newly created Kingdom of Transjordan. Two years later she ceded to Syria a strategic zone in the north which included the Golan Heights. Thus were sown the seeds of two bitter future controversies. The term 'best endeavours' in the Declaration was a favourite Foreign Office platitude which could be stretched to cover even the insensitive efforts of the military government in the inter-war years, and the 'clear understanding that nothing would be done to prejudice the civil and religious rights of existing non-Jewish communities in Palestine' can be seen as a form of words which would doubtless have been employed had the location been Uganda or Uruguay. Taken literally, much depended on exactly what civil rights some of the non-Jewish population had possessed prior to the advent of the Jews. The final sentence reflects the fears of Jews established in the diaspora, that they might be discriminated against or even summarily ejected once there was a national home for them to go to.

According to the terms of the 1918 Armistice, lands formerly occupied by the defeated Turks were placed under the administration of Britain and France as League of Nations Mandates, the exact allocation of territory being the

16

work of Sykes and Picot. The relevant League of Nations text was carefully phrased, on the same lines as the Balfour Declaration. A Jewish Agency (originally the Zionist Organisation itself) was authorised to co-operate with the Mandatory administration in developing public services and national resources. 'It was plain from beginning to end', says Sachar, 'that the League award was framed to protect the Zionist redemptive effort . . . nor was there any doubt that the British Government intended to stand behind the Mandate.' The doubt lies, perhaps, not so much with Britain's intentions as with her understanding of the implications of her commitment. So often what to an outsider looks Machiavellian or treacherous turns out to be merely the fruits of bungling incomprehension. Attlee has looked back on Britain's course of action with characteristic honesty and the benefit of hindsight: 'We'd started something in the Jewish national home after World War One without perceiving the consequences; it was done in a very thoughtless way with people of a different outlook on civilisation suddenly imported into Palestine – a wild experiment that was bound to cause trouble.'

The Jews' first reaction to the Balfour Declaration and even to the Mandate was one of optimism. The 1920s saw the greatest wave yet of immigrants, the Third Aliya as it was called. The bulk of them were from Russia and Eastern Europe, like the First Aliya in the 1880s and the Second Aliya in the early 1900s. This accelerated immigration increased the demand for land and alarmed both the Arab population and also the British administration. Many of the newcomers were members of the Poalei Zion (the Zionist Workers' Front) and had imbibed the 'redemption through toil' philosophy of Arthur Ruppin. They were young and passionately idealistic. Ruppin insisted that Jews must reclaim their own land, hew their own wood and draw their own water, and eschew the use of Arab labour if they were to escape becoming mere colonialists. The early settlers had

17

been unaware of this principle and had established links with the Arabs, usually on a master-and-servant basis. Only a vigorous campaign persuaded the Jewish population (the yishuv) to abandon the use of cheap labour and cultivate self-sufficiency. The price was that they thereby isolated themselves from the bulk of the Arab population. But it took ten or more years under the Mandate umbrella for this to become a major problem.

To give form to their idealism many organised themselves into kibbutzim and moshavim. The kibbutz is a form of pioneering settlement based on collective ownership of property and a communal mode of life. It observes the principles of complete social equality, mutual responsibility and direct democracy. Less uncompromising was the moshav, which retained some private ownership but, like the kibbutz, practised a high degree of mutual aid on collective principles. It was not an easy life, but no one expected it to be. All the settlements fought through years of privation. A few failed; many eventually prospered and today offer their members a comfortable and secure standard of living. The aim was nothing less than to create a new kind of Jew: self-sufficient, resilient, physically tough, spiritually and culturally unshackled. Most of Israel's military and political leaders come from families who immigrated with the Third Aliya and a high proportion of them have passed through kibbutzim. Even those who did not, cannot fail to have been influenced by the zeal and idealism of the collectivist movements. For historically the kibbutz is the foundation of modern Israel, and to the Israeli himself it represents an emotional, intellectual and ideological ideal – that of genuine community and co-operation. For many years before the establishment of the state of Israel, it was the compass which gave direction to the individual Jewish settler, and it still gives stability to a volatile society. Today some 4 per cent of the population live on kibbutzim, yet they produce some 15 per cent of GNP and 16 per cent of

18

Israel's army officers. Many have diversified into industry, especially those in the Negev.

The new settlements needed land. And even where they started with land that was mere swamp and desert, the evicted Arabs looked on with inevitable hatred and envy. When the land began to blossom at the hands of the newcomer with his government loan and his technical ingenuity, not to mention his puritanical appetite for work, the once meagre subsistence holding looked very desirable. The Arabs raided the Jewish crops and settlements. And the Jews claimed the protection of the British military government. But the British Army, much of it fresh from service in India and Egypt, tended to treat the situation as a colonial one involving troublesome natives. Of the two camps they felt more at ease with the Arab side. The Jews were white, yet not British; they bristled with culture and left-wing philosophy; and they behaved as if they assumed the British ought to be on their side all the time. In 1929 there was a serious and concerted wave of Arab riots in the cities of Jerusalem, Haifa and Jaffa, and a veritable massacre of Jews in Hebron. The British Army was too small to restore order and only received reinforcements from Egypt three days after the disturbances were over. The Jews decided they needed their own homeguard defence forces. Individual HaShomer bands, attached to settlements in the north, were organised into a unified defence, the Haganah. The British declared the Haganah illegal, but turned a blind eye most of the time as long as they used their arms (mostly First World War rifles purchased in the local open market) only technically for self-defence. In the wake of the riots the British Government issued a renewed policy statement, known as the Passfield White Paper. This incensed the Jews because it identified the acquisition of land as the main cause of the troubles and suggested that it might be necessary to impose some curbs on immigration. No action was in fact

19

taken on immigration and in 1936 fresh Arab riots broke out and lasted until well into 1938.

Meanwhile, throughout the 1930s, under the umbrella of the British military government, and in the absence of a state machinery, Jewish administrative bodies grew up to organise those uncontroversial areas of activity left open to them. At the same time the various religious factions manoeuvred for power, separately and collectively.

From the outset the Zionist Movement encompassed two conflicting visions of the Jewish national home. One group considered the Jews a nation like any other, entitled to a home of its own where it could work out its own destiny in accordance with one or other of the political and social philosophies prevalent in the nineteenth century, all of which made a clear distinction between religion and the state. Another group saw the Jews as constituting 'a priestly people and a holy nation' and envisaged the Jewish national home as an environment where the nation could once again live fully in accordance with its ancient sacred laws. And between these two groups there was an amorphous centre. The secularists far outnumbered the religious within the Zionist Movement, and even more so within the yishuv, the body of settlers in Palestine. The Mandate indirectly strengthened the hand of the religious faction. In its determination to be even-handed, the Mandatory authorities could only recognise Jewish self-governing institutions if they were matched by a corresponding Arab institution. This was likely to cramp the activities of the Jews. But they found a legal way round the difficulty by utilising the millet system, which the British carried over from Ottoman days. This allowed each religious community a high degree of autonomy. So the Jews built the autonomous institutions they wanted as if they were appendages to the religious bodies they were entitled to set up, and so were able to obtain recognition from the Mandatory government for the whole system. In this way religious courts were set up, together with various other institutions and practices desired by the religious, while the secularists went along with this in order to obtain the political institutions they wanted. The religious parties have taken good care not to lose the valuable ground gained in those pre-state years.

Outside the religious field the key administrative body set up, as early as 1921, was the Histadrut, usually translated as the Workers' Federation. 'Without it,' said Ben Gurion, 'I doubt whether we should have had a state at all.' The avowed purpose of the Histadrut was to arrange all the communal, economic and cultural affairs of the working class of the country for the building of a Labour society. In practical terms one of its first functions was to create jobs on the land for the new immigrants; subsequently came the need to organise unions and job centres to secure employment for an uneven flow of immigrants both in settlements and in the towns. Housing was a top priority, and in the 1930s the Histadrut organised co-operative groups of workers to undertake building and public works, and this soon developed into a special department of public works and building known as Solel Boneh. The Histadrut founded a workers' bank, the Bank HaPoalim, still one of the two major banks in the country, as the credit institution for these operations. Its sick fund, the Kupat Holim, offered a comprehensive medical service, and even today about 70 per cent of the population are affiliated to it. It set up schools, later to be incorporated into the state system, pension funds, training schools and colleges for workers, its own publishing house, HaAm HaSefer, and its own daily newspaper, *Davar*. The Haganah itself was set up by leading members of the Histadrut, and for the first decade of its existence was supervised and led by Histadrut officials. It constituted an autonomous Jewish administration in the absence of a government.

The Histadrut was also a forum of political life. It was, and still is, a self-governing body run by a council elected every four years, and the nascent political parties campaigned for these elections, flexing their muscles for the real political arena of the future. The British Mandatory authorities did not object to this. They were chiefly interested in building roads to keep the country in order, and facilitate the handling of oil along the pipeline from the Gulf to Haifa, and through the extensive port installations they built there. Jerusalem they treated with circumspection, and Tel Aviv they left to the Jews, who made that city the centre for their administration.

Arab riots continued sporadically from 1936 through to mid 1938. During this period, says Allon, 'the Arab guerillas grew in size and strength, and generally the British military forces . . . either showed themselves unwilling to suppress the wave of violence, or when they did attempt to do something, proved their inefficiency by over-reacting.' One notable exception, in Allon's eyes, was Orde Wingate, later to find fame in Burma but then a captain in the British occupying force. As a counter-measure to Arab attacks on the oil pipeline, which were an extension of their long-lasting attacks on Jewish settlements in the Jezreel Valley, Wingate was authorised to enlist Jewish fighters from the settlement police (many of whom were also clandestine members of the Haganah) into his Special Night Squads. These mixed bands of British soldiers and Jewish home-guards fought the Arabs with a refined version of their own guerilla tactics. They also furnished invaluable battle-training for the Jewish fighters, among them two future chiefs of staff, Generals Allon and Dayan. Allon says Wingate's personal example, his stress on exploiting surprise and mobility, his emphasis on giving authority to subordinate officers and training them to be leaders capable of taking command, and regarding them as partners in thinking and action, all these features left their mark on the military thinking and tactics of the Haganah – and consequently on the subsequent Israeli Defence Force (IDF). Wingate's reactions to Zionism were personal and profound and he became something of a folk-hero. To this day in Israel he is the best-loved and most respected Englishman of the Mandate years.

In August 1938 the Arab riots finally ended, with a toll of 6,768 casualties, 2,394 of them Jews, 3,764 Arabs and 610 British. A Royal Commission was set up to investigate the cause of the riots and concluded that they were due to Arab fears engendered by the idea of a Jewish national home in Palestine. It suggested partition, which the Zionist Congress reluctantly accepted on the grounds that half a loaf was better than none. The Arabs, however, rejected partition, and so, eventually, did the British Government, ostensibly on the economic grounds that the Arab part would be in permanent deficit and the Jewish part in permanent surplus, and that wherever the boundaries were set they would not produce two self-supporting states. Perhaps more important were the strategic grounds: with the rise of fascism in Europe and the Italian invasion of Abyssinia and Libya, Palestine could not be allowed to collapse into civil war. Jabotinsky, giving evidence to the Royal Commission in 1938, pronounced a rhetorical *tour de force* which carried a terrible conviction, coming as it did on the eve of Hitler's triumphant advance across Europe. 'Self-expression,' he said, 'the rebuilding of a Hebrew culture, or creating some model community of which the Jewish people could be proud – all that, of course, is important; but as compared with our actual needs and our real position in the world today, all that has rather the character of luxury . . . We are not free agents. We cannot "concede" anything . . . We have to save *millions* . . . When the Arab claim is confronted with our Jewish demand to be saved, it is like the claims of appetite versus the claims of starvation . . . the decisive and terrible balance of need.' Millions were not saved. But hundreds of thousands did escape the Holocaust and many of those found their way to Israel eventually. Menachem Begin was one of them, an ardent young disciple of Jabotinsky. The situation

23

has now changed beyond recognition, but Begin and many of his scarred generation still see the Middle East through Jabotinsky's eyes.

Between Munich in 1938 and the start of the Second World War the following autumn, Britain felt it was imperative to placate the Arab World; there were oil supplies and other investments to be protected, and also the Arabs had to be prevented from gravitating to the Axis powers. So in May 1939 Chamberlain issued a White Paper setting out Britain's revised intentions with regard to Palestine: Britain would organise the transfer of power to an independent Palestine state within the next ten years, and in order to preserve a demographic balance (by which she meant an Arab majority) in the interim, the sale of further land to Jews would be prohibited and a quota imposed on Jewish immigration for the next five years, after which there would be no further Jewish immigration permitted without Arab acquiescence. It meant a foreclosure of any subsequent growth of the Jewish national home, and it sealed off Palestine as a haven for all but an insignificant fraction of Jewish refugees from Europe. Jabotinsky was answered.

The White Paper produced an outcry from Jews and Gentile Zionists everywhere. 'In the short run,' concludes Sachar, 'the pro-Arab orientation of British policy was a defensible act of calculated self-interest. By and large it succeeded in keeping the Arab world quiet, and this was its rationale . . . Its weakness was to be found in the long term, for it destroyed the lingering reality of Anglo-Jewish co-operation and the moral and legal basis upon which the Palestine Mandate had originally been established.' David Ben Gurion led an influential political group urging circumspect militant resistance. 'We must fight the war as if there were no White Paper, he said, and the White Paper as if there were no war.' The Irgun Zvai Leumi (Etzel) went further and bombed government buildings. The Jewish Agency itself organised clandestine immigration (Aliya Bet).

The British retaliated by ordering the surrender of all illegal weapons. The Haganah replied by secretly registering for service all men and women between the ages of eighteen and thirty-five. The immigration issue was enormously emotive. The British occupying forces had become the enemy for thousands of the yishuv.

Yet despite all the bitterness the Jews fought unreservedly with the British in all aspects of the war against Germany. Weizmann expressed their attitude. 'There are higher interests . . . their war is our war.' More than 100,000 Palestinian Jews volunteered for service with the British within the first few days. Some hoped to get back into Europe in British uniform and make contact with fellow Jews marooned there. Many served in the Jewish Brigade in North Africa. Realistic leaders of the Jewish community in Palestine realised that Palestine itself could become a battleground and that it might even, like other territories, be evacuated by the Allies. If this happened, the Jewish community would face two enemies, the Germans and the Arabs. The Jews actually had a plan to collect their entire population of some half a million in the area north of Haifa and make a last-ditch stand. But the moment did not come for such a second Massada. Six million Jews perished in the Holocaust.

Britain steadfastly maintained her immigration restrictions, diverting shiploads of refugees to camps in Cyprus and Mauritius, or even back to their countries of origin, which several of them never reached. Etzel terrorism escalated, with growing support from much of the population. Increasingly aware of their untenable situation, the British set a self-imposed withdrawal deadline of May 1948. In 1946 an Anglo-American Committee of Enquiry produced what is known as the Biltmore Programme. It contained chunks of Jabotinsky rhetoric flanked by careful Foreign Office phraseology and patches of forthright American verbosity. It was liberal on immigration, cautious on the creation of any kind of state in Palestine, Arab or Jewish, and suggested

25

that the Mandate be transferred from Britain to the United Nations. Britain's Foreign Secretary, Ernest Bevin, oppressed by the opprobrium heaped upon him over immigration, announced that he was referring the Palestine problem to the United Nations, which in turn set up a special committee to examine the matter. The UNSCOP (United Nations Special Committee on Palestine) Report recommended the partition of Palestine with economic union, and this was supported by a two-thirds majority, including the United States and Britain. The Jewish Agency accepted it, but the Arabs rejected it. In May 1947 the United Nations Assembly, obviously fearing the worst, passed a resolution on the future government of Palestine. Among other things it considered that 'the present situation in Palestine is one which is likely to impair the general welfare and friendly relations among nations . . .' It noted the United Kingdom's declaration of its intention to withdraw troops by 14 May 1948 and announced that 'if the Security Council considers, in the transitional period, that the situation constitutes a threat to peace it should, under Articles 39 and 41 of the United Nations Charter, exercise the functions assigned to it by this resolution'; in other words send in its own force. By this time Israel was making urgent preparations for the first time to take her destiny into her own hands. For her part she had no illusions about what would happen as soon as the British forces withdrew.

2

The Political Background 1948–83

'At Basle I founded the Jewish state,' wrote Herzl, after the First Zionist Congress in 1896. 'If I were to say this today I should be greeted with laughter. In five years, perhaps, and certainly in fifty years, everyone will see it.' On 15 May, 1948, David Ben Gurion read out Israel's Declaration of Independence to the Provisional Council of State in Tel Aviv, and the Jewish state was indeed founded:

'We . . . representing the Jewish people in the Land of Israel and the Zionist Movement, have assembled on the day of the termination of the British Mandate for Palestine, and by virtue of our natural and historic right and of the Resolution of the General Assembly of the United Nations, do hereby proclaim the establishment of a Jewish state in the land of Israel . . . The state of Israel will be open to Jewish immigration and the ingathering of the exiles.'

This last phrase was, said Golda Meir, the very heart of the proclamation. It went on to pledge the future state

'to uphold the full social and political equality of all its citizens without distinction of religion, race or sex . . . Even in the midst of the violent attacks launched against us, we call upon the Arab inhabitants of Israel to keep the peace and play their part in building the state on the basis of full and equal citizenship and due representation in all its institutions, provisional and permanent. We extend the hand of peace and good neighbourliness to all the states around us and to their peoples, and we call

27

on them to co-operate with the independent Jewish nation in its land. The state of Israel is prepared to make its contribution to the progress of the Middle East as a whole.'

Like most such proclamations this one contained a mixture of defiance and pious hopes; the more so since, at the moment it was being read out, troops from three of Israel's neighbours were actually waging active war inside her territory. As Berl Katznelson, the great secular philosopher of the early yishuv, was wont to say: 'The world does not exist on a *tabula rasa*; we are not born outside history.'

The run-up to independence had not been smooth. In November 1947, under the dual pressure of Arab demands and an uneasy Anglo-American reaction to the Jewish refugee problem, UNSCOP had come up with a plan for partition. One has only to look at the map to see how unrealistic the plan was, even with the proviso that it would be supervised by an international commission under the jurisdiction of the United Nations Security Council. With the already existing level of informal hostilities between Arabs and Jews, the United Nations recommendation, and its acceptance by the Jewish leaders, could be seen as little more than a formal gesture. Ben Gurion accepted it on the grounds that it would at least concede some territory where Jews could go as of right.

There was an action group in the country who were impatient at what they considered the naïvety of the Jewish Agency in playing along with these negotiations. Throughout 1947 and 1948 a group led by Menachem Begin organised a campaign of high melodrama. Begin had escaped to Israel from a Siberian concentration camp in 1943 and his hatred of the British reached white heat over their heel-tapping about admitting immigrants into Palestine. With no temper at that time for statesmanship, he placed himself at the head of a group who felt compelled to hasten events along by a campaign of terrorism. They called themselves the Irgun Tzvai Leumi, known in Israel by its acronym Etzel. Many moderate Jews tended to be inhibited about denouncing Etzel by the fact that many of its members were religious zealots, while the Mandate restrictions, which were their avowed target, were an exposed nerve for all Jews without exception. Begin's book, *The Revolt*, published in 1952, paints the Etzel terrorist campaign as some sort of Bar Kochba Jewish revolt which culminated in the creation of the state of Israel. It lacks historical perspective or political wisdom and is suffused with purple rhetoric. Nevertheless, when he broadcast a message to his supporters on the Day of Independence, he dedicated his organisation unequivocally to the service of the new state, 'where there is no need for a Hebrew underground. In the state of Israel we shall be soldiers and builders. We shall respect its government, for it is our government . . .' And so it was, eventually.

Ben Gurion accepted the UNSCOP partition plan, but the Arabs rejected it. Before May 1948 a military force assembled in Syria and started to infiltrate from the north, and an Egyptian force advanced from the south across the Negev Desert and cut off towns there from the rest of Palestine. As the Syrian Army moved southwards the roads linking the main cities of Haifa, Tiberias and Tel Aviv were under constant attack, and Jerusalem was virtually cut off from its source of supplies, Tel Aviv. And all this before the deadline for the withdrawal of British troops. The British record in this period can hardly be a source of pride, whatever official policy may have been, and Sykes calls it one of mischievous incompetence. Foreign Secretary Bevin's lack of sympathy with the Jews is well-documented, and the Foreign Office seems to have done nothing to temper his irritation. While the British Army openly handed over arms and fortified camps to the Arabs, it continued systematically to disarm the Haganah. The Jews had to train in secret, and what weapons they possessed had to be imported illegally and hidden in scattered settlements. Since the British Army was still theoretically the force of law and order in the land, the Haganah had to restrict its retaliation against Arab attacks to static defence. Yet the date had been fixed for the end of the Mandate, and realistically the Haganah leaders had to plan for some sort of concerted campaign as soon as the British withdrew from the territory. It seems likely that the British simply assumed the Arabs would win; though they can hardly have thought through all the implications of that eventuality.

Jewish forces on the eve of independence have been estimated at about 3,000 youths in the Palmach (the Haganah commando group), some 5,000–6,000 Etzel and Lech'i troops (Lech'i were better known in the British press as the Stern Gang, after their leader), and somewhere between 21,000 and 45,000 Haganah reserves consisting of partially trained and ludicrously ill-equipped men, women and teenagers. By the end of hostilities in January 1949 they had lost 6,000 dead out of a population of 600,000.

It has been suggested that the Zionists had not foreseen the speed with which they would be thrown on their own, politically and militarily, and that, preoccupied with their campaign against the British, they had not anticipated the gravity of the Arab military threat. But that was not true of Ben Gurion and the group of emergent military and political leaders around him. They had been intensifying their efforts to obtain arms ever since Ben Gurion's first fund-raising visit to America in 1945. 'What did we have?' asks Golda Meir, who was one of that group, and who was despatched on a similar errand two days after independence. 'Not much of anything – and even that is an exaggeration. A few thousand rifles, an assortment of other firearms, but on 14 May 1948 not a single cannon or tank, though we had all of nine planes (never mind that only one had two engines). The machinery for making arms had been bought abroad . . . but couldn't be brought into Israel until the British left, and then it had to be assembled and run in.' Since 1945, in fact, Haim Slavine had been visiting junk-yards and factories from coast to coast in America buying up surplus war material and machine-tools. Ehud Avriel set up a whole clandestine organisation for purchasing and shipping Czech arms to the Haganah by devious routes. All this is worth recording because it was the first but not the last time Israel was to scour markets for arms, while countries she considered a threat to her existence seemed to be finding the going easier. The resulting siege mentality has not left Israel since.

There is no doubt that Israel faced the serious threat of annihilation in those first days and weeks, and neither Britain nor the United States had yet decided she was a horse they were officially backing. Today, with the Entebbe reputation she has acquired for 'creating facts', it is hard to realise that in 1948 the world's image of the Jews was of bewildered masses of humanity being herded apparently passively to their deaths in Nazi Germany. What value could their new state possibly have in the global politics of the Middle East? It took nineteen years, until the Six-Day War, for Israel to make her mark on Western consciousness. But the generation of 1948 has never forgiven the world for its former indifference, and that has been built into Israeli consciousness, mellowed with the years but not eradicated. 'If we do not fight for ourselves who will fight for us?'

Israel won her War of Independence to the extent that she was not driven, as the Arabs had threatened, into the sea. But it was a visceral struggle shared by every member of the yishuv. The key to the outcome was certainly not Israeli military strength, but rather that in the actual fighting all semblance of a united command over the invading Arab forces disintegrated. In the north, the Syrian troops failed to make headway once the Israelis were in a position to organise their forces openly. The Iraqi Army, further south, failed to cross the Jordan. The Egyptians got within fifteen miles of Tel Aviv but ran out of steam. Eventually the most coherent attack was that launched into the West Bank area

31

by the Transjordanian Arab Legion under the command of the high-ranking British military character known as Glubb Pasha. The fiercest fighting was on the Tel Aviv-Jerusalem road where hundreds of Jewish lives were lost keeping supplies moving to the besieged Jewish population in Jeruslaem. Yitzhak Rabin, later Prime Minister but in 1948 a young Palmach officer, listened to the independence speeches on the radio in a kibbutz on the Jerusalem Road where the battle was already raging. The British Army continued its withdrawal to meet the deadline of 14 May.

The United Nations estimated that over 725,000 Arabs fled from Palestine between April and December 1949. The leaders of the Arab community were the first to go and left the rest without guidance or any political institutions. Many refugees believed they would soon be able to return to their homes once Israel had been destroyed. Some 160,000 Arabs either remained in Jewish-occupied territory or returned there during 1949. But there is no doubt that at a certain moment the Arab population panicked, and this panic was fuelled by one documented instance of reprisals by Jewish forces which Israel has remembered with shame ever since. When the Arab village of Deir Yassin, on the road to Jerusalem, was captured by an Etzel group, its 200 inhabitants, men, women and children, were murdered, mutilated and thrown into a well.

The deed was at once repudiated by the Haganah and by the Israeli Government, which was shortly afterwards to have its own showdown with Etzel; but that could not undo the damage. Arabs poured out of the cities in Jewish-occupied areas and many peasants also left their small-holdings. In the heat of the conflict, intimidation no doubt encouraged panic.

When the conflict was over the Israelis called on the Arabs to return to their property. Few did so. It was not an offer left open for long. Israel needed land and housing for the high tide of immigrants from Europe. The main areas from

32

which the Arabs fled were the north-west corner (whence they went to Lebanon and Syria) and a triangle between Tel Aviv, Jerusalem and Gaza, from which they crowded south to the Gaza Strip or eastwards into the West Bank. About 10 per cent crossed the Jordan into Transjordan. The host populations had neither the wealth nor the will to absorb this influx, so they settled in large refugee camps. These camps, transformed over the years into poor townships, bred a second generation of rootless Arabs, liable to be whipped up into resentment by vengeful political factions.

It was a thorn planted in Israel's side which festered and would not go away; a focus of hatred for her Arab neighbours and a continuous blot on her international image. For a country peopled with refugees to be saddled with the international responsibility for a major refugee problem was psychologically hard for the average Israeli to contend with; but having individually risen phoenix-like from the situation themselves, they have been torn between guilt and exasperation at the example on their doorstep.

In 1949 this problem was in its infancy and Israel was too busy putting her own house in order to appreciate the implications. In January 1949 the United Nations Security Council, after repeated calls for a cease-fire, managed to engineer a permanent armistice. By this time the Israeli Army had opened the road to Jerusalem and driven the Arab forces back well beyond the frontiers in the north and south envisaged by the UNSCOP report. An armistice was negotiated at Rhodes where fresh frontiers were drawn for Israel which included a smaller Gaza Strip and a reduced West Bank area with a generous Israeli corridor through to Jerusalem. Jerusalem itself was divided, with the whole of the old city placed in the Arab sector and occupied by the Jordanian Arab Legion along with the rest of the West Bank area. These could not, by any stretch of the imagination, be called secure frontiers, but for the moment it seemed enough that there was no longer an immediate external

33

threat to the existence of the state. Israel was a state in need of a new set of institutions, a legislature, a judiciary, an independent political leadership and, as a first priority, parliamentary elections.

Owing to the peculiar circumstances preceding its birth, Israel had fully fledged political parties and a formally representative provisional government ready and waiting in the wings, and she had a political leader of quite exceptional stature, David Ben Gurion. 'In Ben Gurion,' wrote Shimon Peres, who was close to him for the last thirty years of his life, 'the two most important ingredients of leadership were combined; earthy realism and sky-scraping vision.' Another associate described him as a 'man in whom an impulsive wisdom is blended with a deep sense of morality.' Charisma he had, as everyone who knew him agreed, but of quite a different kind from Weizmann. Each belonged to his era.

Ben Gurion had arrived in Palestine from Poland in 1906. He studied law under the Turks, and served in the Jewish Battalion of the British Army in the First World War. He worked on the land, with the Zionist Organisation and in the Histadrut. He was in the thick of the action throughout the years 1917 to 1948. His vision was the creation of a unified Jewish people out of the disparate immigrant populations. This he achieved, in his day, both politically and militarily. He coaxed the fragmented parties and pressure groups of the secular left into a semblance of political unity in the form of the Mapai party, born in 1930, out of a handful of kibbutz and moshav workers' parties. Even so, it was not until 1965, after a traumatic boiling up and spilling over of surviving undercurrents, that Ben Gurion's work was completed and the remaining socialist group, Mapam, consented to participate in the formation of the Israeli Labour party.

Ben Gurion's second healing and unifying achievement was in the military sphere. With clear-sighted courage he challenged the potential military and paramilitary pressure groups and insisted they sink their identities in the new Israeli Defence Force. The nature of this problem is examined in a later chapter. The key to its solution lay in the loyal response he met from all ranks of all parts of the fighting forces. His short, stocky figure, rugged, rocklike and totally lacking in ceremony, epitomised the Israel of 1948. He was then at the height of his power, universally respected as a person and virtually unchallenged as political leader of the new state. Weizmann, it is true, was made President, but he was by then old and tired and a little out of touch with the post-war spirit. He rarely left his home at Rehovot, in the foothills outside Tel Aviv, and tended to be consulted on history rather than policy-making. The presidency has always been a prestigious but largely ceremonial position. It was Ben Gurion who handled the delicate matter of setting up the new framework of sovereign government. In point of fact the smoothness of the operation was due less to his positive action than to his forbearance, even his resistance, in face of the positive activists.

For the duration of the War of Independence the Peoples Council (Va'ad Leumi), which since 1920 had been elected to administer Jewish affairs under the Mandate, simply became the Provisional Government of Israel. Administrative departments already existed, operating under the auspices of the Va'ad Leumi and the Jewish Agency, to cover health, religious affairs, finance, trade and industry, etc. and these merely changed their names to Ministries and took over from the Mandatory government. As soon as the war ended, in January 1949, the first elections were held. The party list voting system, which had been used for decades for Va'ad Leumi elections among the yishuv, was naturally continued, and an already well-established array of parties entered the campaign. Ben Gurion, leader of Mapai, the largest party in the resulting assembly, formed the first government, and this was a coalition with three other

35

parties, including a group calling itself the United Religious Front. A pattern was established.

The intention was that the National Assembly produced by these elections would draw up a constitution. But Israel was in no mood for protracted constitution-making and Ben Gurion demonstrated his wisdom by letting the situation ride. He fended off ambitious but controversial draft constitutions, and pointed to the example of Britain, functioning for centuries without a formal written constitution. The Constituent Assembly simply became, nominally, the first Parliament or Knesset. To this day Israel has a single chamber of 120 members, elected nationwide by a party-list system of proportional representation. There are no constituencies. Each party list contains up to 120 names, in an order of precedence decided by the party's central committee. The voter votes for the party whose programme and leaders he prefers. It is a simple practical system for a country of Israel's size: the land would fit comfortably into a triangle made by London, Oxford and York.

'The intention', says Sachar, somewhat lyrically, 'was to combine the best of the Continental system with the noblest of the British . . . a powerful legislature in law but not in practice, and a dominant cabinet in practice, although not in law'. The Prime Minister, for example, does not choose his Cabinet; its members are nominated by the coalition parties. They need not even be Knesset members, although most of them are. The Prime Minister cannot dismiss a Minister, not even one from his own party on his own authority, nor can he dissolve the Knesset and precipitate a general election. Even if the Knesset votes no confidence in a Cabinet, this does not necessarily herald a general election; all that may happen is that the President will invite another party leader to form a new government, although the likelihood is that any such new government would not wait too long before seeking confirmation in a general election. But neither the President nor the Prime Minister can dissolve the Knesset. Only the Knesset itself can do that and call a general election before a government has run its full four-year term. One important source of strength to a British Prime Minister is not available to his Israeli counterpart; this is the convention of collective Cabinet responsibility, according to which all Cabinet members (together with about a hundred lesser government office-holders in Parliament) publicly stand by the collective decisions of the Government, even though they may not privately agree with them and may even have fought (in a minority position) for quite different policies *before* those Cabinet decisions were taken. Israelis have never adopted, or even comprehended, this British practice. Their instinct has been for hard bargaining and reluctant compromise, often with maximum publicity to make sure the electorate is aware of the valiance of the struggle. Such a system demands vigorous and assertive leadership.

The President is elected by the Knesset, for five years and a maximum of two consecutive terms, and he presides but does not rule. His only important function is that of designating who shall form a government, and here his choice will be determined by which political figure can gain the support of the Knesset. Usually this has been the leader of the largest political grouping, but in recent years the two main coalition groupings, the right-wing Likud and the left-wing Labour Alignment, have been running neck and neck. This situation has sometimes placed the President in the limelight in a time of crisis, but so far has not thrust important constitutional decisions upon him. Both Navon and Herzog were in fact elected to the presidency in the teeth of Begin's preferred candidate simply because they had broad support in the Knesset.

Ben Gurion's long initial term of office saw the new system through its teething troubles and weaned it into permanence. When, for example, in 1951, his government was defeated in the Knesset due to a stand made by the religious

37

group in his coalition, he at once resigned with his Cabinet. The Knesset then drafted legislation to cover this eventuality and establish the principle of general elections every four years. After the election Ben Gurion formed a fresh government with an enhanced majority. In this, and much of its subsequent evolution, the Knesset followed a British precedent. It has a Speaker, elected by the Knesset, who, with an all-party presidium, timetables the work of the chamber; there are three readings for Bills, with debate and committee stages; the legislative procedure concludes with signature by the Prime Minister, the Minister responsible and the President of the State. There are two official languages, Hebrew and Arabic, with simultaneous translation available. The distinctive Israeli characteristic has always been an influential committee system, which has detracted from the importance of debates on the floor of the Knesset. There is no quorum for a debate, and minor bills have been known to be put to the vote in the presence of as few as eight members. The bulk of the Knesset's work is carried out in the nine specialist committees. Composition of these is proportionate to party strength in the Knesset itself, and it is here, under the chairmanship of the appropriate Minister, that policy is made and fought over. One problem is that numbers in some of the minority parties are so small that they do not even suffice to man all the central committees. In fact the Knesset itself has tended to be almost exclusively a club for the ruling élites of the various parties. Rather than being a training ground for future leaders, on the British model, it is the stamping ground for small party oligarchies. This situation is further aggravated by the fact that certain ministries have become the preserves of certain parties. For instance, the religious group have insisted through the years on being allocated the portfolios of Social Welfare and Home Affairs, in order to keep their grip on policy-making in those areas. There is no need to stress the obvious importance of the Judicial and the Foreign Affairs Committees, but the key body is the Defence and Foreign Affairs Committee, which is very powerful indeed and is the object of the sort of criticism levelled in Britain against certain Cabinet Committees, or even that elusive animal, the 'inner Cabinet'.

Israel's party system, does not bear analogy with either the European or American patterns. The explanation lies in its roots, which go back well before the establishment of an independent government. The early yishuv was a pioneer society, composed mostly of Western Jews imbued with early socialist idealism and a strong sense of the dignity of labour. In the absence of an established ruling class or any important vested interest, social or economic, the emphasis was not anti-capitalist but on the need to create work for workers; and given the Mandate situation the emphasis had to be concentrated at grass-roots level. Similarly, the economic and welfare machinery of the Histadrut did not grow as an arm of a government department; it evolved as an umbrella organisation for grass-roots activity, strongly worker-orientated.

A difference which British observers often stress is the lack of an 'organised opposition' in the form of a Shadow Cabinet waiting in the wings to offer the electorate an alternative government. But it must be realised that coalition governments in general to not lend themselves to this pattern, and Britain, not Israel, is the odd man out in this respect. In any case British adversary politics have not been without their critics in the 1970s and '80s.

Israel has her own system of political checks and balances; between Committee and Cabinet, Cabinet and Knesset, major and minor coalition member parties. All coalitions have depended on the support of a minority religious group which has taken a consistently hard line on certain religious and social issues, including, in the 1980s, fundamental questions like settlements in the occupied territories. This was just as true throughout the twenty-four years of socialist coalition government as it has been since 1977 during the period of Begin's right-wing coalition. No doubt this situation could have been modified in the early years had there existed the political will to do so. But Israelis, at all levels, distrust political power, and have been content to place successive governments in chronic insecurity. So far this political insecurity has been masked by recurrent wars, when power and the national will have necessarily been concentrated on the military effort. Nothing unites a country like a threat, real or imagined, to its survival. Yet it must be said that at no time in the first twenty-five years could an Israeli government be accused of playing the war card to capture the electorate.

The wars did, however, seriously distort the machinery of government by bestowing prominence on defence matters. It was not unnatural for Ben Gurion, in the initial months after independence, to take the Defence portfolio himself; as head of government Defence was his over-riding preoccupation in those early months. But even after the War of Independence had ended, there was a certain amount of jostling for power within the armed forces, and Ben Gurion felt his hand was still needed there. Thereafter, throughout the 1950s and '60s, war, arms procurement and preparations for possible future war remained a constant preoccupation. This syndrome will be examined in a later chapter.

For the first twenty years, from 1948 to 1968, the political scene was dominated by a remarkably stable élite group, sometimes simply known as the sareinu (our ministers). Some of these were old guard, in their fifties or over: Ben Gurion himself, Moshe Sharett, who was Foreign Affairs Minister until 1956; Levi Eshkol who was Finance Minister from 1952 to 1964 when he succeeded Ben Gurion as Prime Minister; Haim Shapira who dominated Social Affairs for twenty years either from that Ministry or from the Interior Ministry on behalf of the religious bloc; and Pinhas Sapir, 'the human avalanche' as Eban called him, whose area was

Economic Affairs. In harness with the old guard, some would say for too long, were the Young Turks of the second, Israeli-bred generation: Yigal Allon, Palmach leader and hero of the War of Independence; Moshe Dayan, star of the Six-Day War in 1967; Abba Eban, who spent many years burnishing Israel's image at the United Nations before becoming Foreign Minister in 1968; and Shimon Peres, technocrat *par excellence*, consummate politician and Ben Gurion's chosen long-term dauphin, although he did not find that time and the tide of public opinion were on his side. These were the power élite which survived more or less intact through twelve Cabinets and five general elections.

Some people see 1967 as a watershed in Israeli politics. Eshkol, they say, was the 'last of the just' and his passing marked the end of Israel's heroic age. Like most of the sareinu he had passed through kibbutz and Haganah on his way up to the Cabinet, and he inspired affection and respect in all who worked with him. 'We wanted to build Israel with our bare hands,' he used to say. Other observers attribute great significance to the Six-Day War. Israel, they say, stared destruction in the face, and this fear concentrated the minds of the diverse factions and brought them together in a new pattern. Some of the old guard were thought to be tarnishing the new-born image with too much wheeling and dealing, and keeping their cards too close to the chest. Golda Meir, Prime Minister from 1969 to 1974, decided most Defence and Foreign Affairs matters in her kitchen Cabinet, while domestic party issues were handled by the Finance Minister, Pinhas Sapir, 'the great fixer'. The Knesset, and indeed the Cabinet as a whole body, was in danger of becoming little more than a rubber stamp. People talked about the 'Levantinisation' of the country – a prospect abhorred alike by Ben Gurion and the young technocrats, who took very seriously the challenge of guiding Israel's healthy economic development.

A manifestation of this period of malaise, and one which

41

occupies inordinate space in the chronicles of the 1960s, is the Lavon Affair. It needs putting in perspective. It began as a sordid little spy scandal in 1954, when an Israeli Intelligence officer in Cairo was authorised by someone then in the Defence Ministry, perhaps even by the Minister, Lavon, to carry out a campaign of bomb outrages in such a manner that the Americans would blame the Egyptians, who would be duly diplomatically alienated. There was only one actual casualty, the operation was blown, two Israeli agents were sentenced to death and hanged, two escaped and the rest served sentences in Egyptian prisons. It was only eleven years later, in 1965, that this story and its infinite ramifications was leaked to the press. The object, it would seem, was to cut Lavon down to size; he was a man who made enemies easily. Ben Gurion, who had been Prime Minister in 1954 and was convinced that the honour of his administration was at stake, started a witch-hunt. No one seemed particularly fond of Lavon as the saga drew out, and the sole importance of the Lavon Affair was that it acted as a catalyst in Israeli politics in 1965.

The 'Young Turks', Peres and his friends, may have thought they perceived in it a way of breaking open the citadel of power. To them one way forward appeared to be to start a new party, outside the closed yet disaffected ranks of the old Mapai group. They launched RAFI. It was to embody a fresh technocratic approach while remaining faithful to the true ideals of the left, which, it claimed, had been compromised by some of the old leaders. It was uphill work. The left was at a low ebb, Ben Gurion was experiencing a personal crisis at Sde Boker, his kibbutz in the Negev, and Peres' heart was not in the new venture. The 1965 elections merely proved what many people had suspected: that RAFI was a false trail. It won only 10 seats while the old Mapai held 45. The rising star in the political firmament proved instead to be Gahal, a new right-wing Herut-Liberal bloc, which won 26 seats.

The wind of change was indeed blowing, but from a largely unforeseen quarter. For seventeen years there had been consensus about the basic issues facing the state: immigration and the settlement of new immigrants, and a socialist framework of institutions to support a vulnerable, developing population and economy. But after 1965, and even more so in the atmosphere of greater national security after the 1967 victory, the old political oligarchy ceased to mask a changing reality.

The first change occurred when Gahal joined the wartime government of national unity which Ben Gurion was persuaded to come back and lead in 1967. This conferred on Gahal a new respectability. For the first time there was evidence of an anti-socialist front, the beginnings of an organised parliamentary opposition. Gahal exerted its growing influence on the side of the hawks, and encouraged greater toughness and reliance on the IDF.

Secondly, there was a growing threat to the economic health of the country. Money and resources devoted to arms were inevitably subtracted from the total available for consumption and social investment. This problem was only in its infancy in 1967.

Thirdly, and most fundamental of all, was the important demographic change taking place. In the period 1952 to 1958 about 38,000 Oriental Jews came to Israel from Yemen and Iraq, while another 142,000 North African Jews came from Morocco, Algeria and Tunisia. Quite apart from the formidable economic challenge of providing housing, employment and education for them, they could obviously not be absorbed into the existing state without in the long run changing its very nature. In 1967 the demands of the new immigrants were mostly economic and social; ten years later their demands would be political as well.

These were serious changes in society, yet rather than face up to the new issues the old parties and alliances simply

43

closed ranks and sought to avert the uncertainties of division. Unity tended to become an end in itself. Ominous signs of crumbling unity were already visible in the 1973 elections, when Labour lost 5 seats and, more significantly, the right-wing Likud gained 13. Labour remained in power, but the writing was on the wall. It is debatable whether any action by Labour's leaders then could have averted its decline in the years that followed. The fact is they were so preoccupied with a personal contest for leadership within the party that they failed to respond positively enough to a change of spirit in the country. On the one hand there was Yitzhak Rabin, ex-Chief of Staff and hero of the Six-Day War. He had retired from the Army in 1967 and spent five years as ambassador in Washington before entering politics in 1973 and the same year being chosen party leader. He owed his success to his war record of impeccable administrative efficiency and to a reputation for uncompromising integrity. The party rated this quality highly at the time. On the other hand it became evident that Rabin lacked both the charisma and the political acumen and dynamism needed to reinvigorate the party. Shimon Peres, the dauphin and experienced *apparatchik* with a lifetime of party wheeling and dealing behind him, became a formidable rival. The contrast of personalities could hardly have been more striking. The two men were the same age, both products of one of Ruppin's agricultural schools in the 1930s, but whereas Rabin had gone straight from pioneer youth movement to Haganah, and thence to the Palmach and an Army career as an obvious high-flier, Peres had gravitated to the political centre, to the Haganah headquarters in Tel Aviv and thence to Ben Gurion's secretariat and the Defence Department. The two men were, and still are, too different in their basic chemistry to tolerate each other. Rabin has always felt Peres was subtly undermining his position, whether as general, party leader or Prime Minister. Peres has seen Rabin as a political innocent, inhibited by a desire for moral purity from taking the deci-

44

sions incumbent on a political leader. Both are highly intelligent, perceptive men who are convinced that the accession to power of the other would be against the best interests of the party and of the nation.

There is no doubt that the introspective in-fighting between these two men contributed to the defeat of the Labour party in the 1977 elections. For one thing, as the election loomed Peres challenged Rabin for the second time for the party leadership. For the second time Rabin won, by a small majority; but then a rather hypocritical little scandal broke out over his head. It was revealed that his wife had kept a bank account open in Washington from the days when they were resident there at the embassy. Although he was by no means alone in doing this, it was against Israeli law. Since spotless integrity was Rabin's strong card, he felt obliged, after this tarnishing little revelation, to resign as party leader. Peres stepped into his shoes just in time to fight a doomed election.

Other factors also contributed to the result – high inflation, high taxation, labour unrest, and a series of other last-minute scandals which only set the seal on the electorate's estimate of the ruling oligarchy of 1977: 'an arrogant, self-serving, unresponsive leadership, corrupted by fifty years of power', was one critic's verdict.

Let us go back and trace the progress of the Likud bloc which emerged in strength in 1973 and steadily occupied the centre ground as Labour vacated it.

In 1949, when Etzel officially ceased to exist, Begin had formed the Herut party. It was pro-Western, capitalist, and it supported the historic borders of Eretz Israel covering the whole of 1917 Palestine on both sides of the Jordan, justifying this nationalistic stance with an appeal to orthodox Judaism. Herut concentrated on winning the support of the new immigrants, who, in the 1950s, were mostly from Eastern Europe and untouched by liberal socialism. After

45

the mass immigrations from Yemen, Iraq and North Africa in the early 1960s, Herut also sought the support of these new uncommitted voters. In 1964 Herut made common cause with the Independent Liberals ('Liberal' here being entirely free from British connotations), forming a right-centre bloc known by its Hebrew acronym Gahal. In the elections of 1965 and 1969 Gahal gained 26 seats. In the 1973 elections two small right-wing parties, Achdut and Le'am, joined with Gahal to form a new centre-right bloc called Likud (Unity). Gahal and the other members of the block would henceforth keep their individual party structures but present a joint list for the elections. A notable driving force behind the formation of this new bloc was General Ariel Sharon, newly arrived in politics.

As regards actual policies, Labour already occupied all the desirable ground: a hard line on defence, more secure frontiers than Israel had ever known before, the Galili Plan for massive investment in developing the West Bank territory and Gaza, more Jewish settlements on the Golan Heights, in the Jordan Valley and around East Jerusalem. What more could any right-wing opposition group offer?

The answer was, a focus for proliferated discontent. The poor, mainly Oriental new immigrants felt the pinch of rising prices and housing shortages; the self-employed middle class were impatient of socialist policies and were attracted to the free-enterprise aspects of Likud. Add to this the sense of disillusion at the petty corruption and in-fighting inside the Labour Alignment revealed by two of the dirtiest election campaigns in Israel's history, and it is not at all surprising the Likud won 43 seats in 1977. The Labour Alignment also won 43 seats, but they had made too many enemies and the coalition-building process went against them. When they saw which way the wind was blowing the group of religious parties joined the Likud-led coalition, and ex-General Sharon, recently converted to politics by a check in his military career-expectations, offered Likud the support of

46

the two elected members of his newly formed Shlomzion party. In all, Begin could count on the backing of 62 out of 120 Knesset members. The scale had tipped.

Constitutionally there was no reason why the Labour Alignment should not have agreed to join a government of national unity in 1977 under Begin. Israel does not traditionally have a two-party system of alternative government like Britain; but just as Likud had grown up as an extra-coalition party grouping in opposition, so now did the Labour Alignment swing into opposition. In any case Peres did not envisage a long stay out in the cold. But events outside the party arena intervened.

In May 1977, just a month after Likud came to power, President Sadat of Egypt made his historic visit to Jerusalem. It was not an occasion set up overnight, or even in a month, but it was Begin who reaped the spin-off in terms of prestige and apparent statesmanship. The ensuing peace negotiations, later spurred on by the American initiative of President Carter and the Camp David Agreement, brought Begin fluctuating credit as they waxed and waned. The fact remained, however, that it was Begin, the mystical patriot, who forced on some of his own unwilling supporters the withdrawal from occupied Sinai in accordance with the Camp David Agreement. It was, by all accounts, an historic moment, and one of considerable public emotional impact.

To its discredit, the Labour Alignment in opposition in the next four years made very little impression. In 1981, at the end of its first four-year term of office, Likud could still claim to be the 'government capable of governing', and the electorate was still ready to believe it. Some would say it is only outside events, possibly skilfully stage-managed, which have given outside observers and an inexperienced section of the electorate an impression of strong leadership. Attention has been distracted from the bankruptcy of domestic policies and the lack of balanced central leadership within the Cabinet. The fact is, Begin must preserve a delicate

47

balance, not only between the parties of the Likud coalition, but also between the factions within the disguised coalition which is his own party, Herut. An Israeli Prime Minister, it must be remembered, has to work with the ministers chosen by his coalition partners. He cannot choose and he cannot dismiss. Even within Herut the constituent groups must be fairly represented; not to mention those individuals who have set their sights on one particular portfolio, such as Defence, and are unwilling to settle for less. Add to this the assumption that certain parties shall control certain areas of policy, and you have an acute example of political vested interests: Culture, Education and Social Affairs for the religious parties; Finance and Economic Affairs for the Liberals, etc. Yaniv and Shlaim have said: 'One of the most difficult tasks facing Begin is that of restraining all the ministers – the civilians as well as the insubordinate former generals – in a government which, through feuds, rivalries and constant bickering, has lost its credibility in the eyes of its supporters as well as in the eyes of the general public . . . Within two years the Liberals' free-market policies produced a situation verging on anarchy and an economic crisis of monumental proportions with runaway inflation, a massive trade deficit and declining investment. This economic record not only destroyed the confidence of the Israeli public in the ability of the government to manage the country's domestic affairs, but also entails growing dependence on the United States, and hence greater vulnerability to American pressure.' Worse could not have been said of the Labour Alignment on the eve of the fateful 1977 elections. Yet opinion polls continue to show that Begin has a clear majority of the electorate behind him. No wonder the same critics spare no sympathy for the opposition either. 'Like the Bourbons of France, the Labour party leaders seem to have learnt nothing and to have forgotten nothing during the enforced period of their exile from power.'

When, in the summer of 1982, Israel launched Operation

48

Peace for Galilee, the government's motives and aims were apparently mixed. It was the most politically divisive war Israel had ever engaged in. All parties recognised the fact that it was a tactical war and not one on which the survival of the state depended in the short run. Also it would seem that all parties were agreed on the advisability of a limited operation to make the northern border more secure, even if that meant unilaterally creating a twenty-mile wide demilitarised buffer zone. But right and left parted company over the extent of the operation and the advisability or feasibility of such an ambitious goal as a partitioned Lebanon, administered by Syria and Israel, on either side of a 'Free City of Beirut'. At any rate even if their long-term aims were grounded in a similar vision of political realities, they envisaged very different routes for attaining them.

Labour started to protest as soon as the twenty-mile agreed line had been passed. The ensuing bombardment of Beirut brought Labour leaders to their feet in the Knesset and Labour voters out on the streets in public demonstrations. The much-publicised 'Peace Now' movement was but the tip of an iceberg. Labour military leaders saw carefully nurtured plans for a relatively peaceful diplomatic evolution in the area, blasted ten years out of reach. For the military establishment is not monolithic in Israel. Peri may very properly talk of the 'permeability of the boundaries between the military and politics' so that 'the Army has never had to resort to coercive means to ensure that its views are listened to or acted upon'; but at the same time alternative political allegiance has led to alternative currents of military thinking in some fields. The fact that General Sharon was Chief of Staff and Defence Minister in 1982 did not preclude an important section of the highest-ranking reserve officers in all walks of life from disagreeing vehemently and publicly with his conduct of Operation Peace for Galilee. In Israel the political opposition is not silenced by the closing of military ranks, even in wartime. The permeability of political

49

and military functions works both ways. It says something important about the persistent health of democracy in Israel that a hawkish right-wing government in a state of war should have been forced by public opinion to submit to the unquestionably impartial scrutiny of the Kahane Commission of Enquiry into the Phalangist massacres of Palestinians in the Sabra and Chatilla Camps, that both Begin and some of his closest associates should have been publicly criticised by that Commission in the highest moral terms, and that Begin should nevertheless have remained Prime Minister for the simple reason that the parliamentary opposition realised that his Likud government would return to power with an enhanced majority if they forced a dissolution. The democratic process, at least, came out of the affair with credit. All the greater, then, were the heart-searchings of those who, in European terms, would perhaps be called the liberal left.

'Security is no longer the major concern,' wrote Rabbi David Goldberg. 'The issue is quite simply what kind of Israel do her people, and Jews world-wide, want?' Labour's misgivings about the war focused attention on the widening distance between Ashkhenazim and Sephardim, between European and Oriental Jews, the latter being a growing proportion of the population and of the electorate. 'Already the two sides are lining up. Behind Mr Begin and General Sharon is a sinister levy of West Bank settlers, Army officers who resent being the scapegoat for political errors, underprivileged Sephardim, and all those who calculate that annexation can be made acceptable, provided that the Holocaust is invoked to deter criticism, and anyone who expresses reservations is accused of anti-Semitism. On the other side are all those who retain, however falteringly, the vision of a democratic Zionist state founded on humane Jewish values and trying to reach accommodation with Arab neighbours. Those values have steadily been eroded over the past five years by the we-are-the-masters-now cockiness of the Likud party. Nor has the me-too-ism of Mr Peres on such issues as negotiating with the PLO or recognising Palestinian nationalism offered a clear alternative to Mr Begin's inflexibility.' Both the rhetorical flourish of this indictment and its overall pessimistic conclusion capture a broad spectrum of thoughtful opinion among Israelis in 1983. Begin has been accused of putting territory above people and spiritual pride above the moral quality of life. There is no sign of the breaking of the political mould.

3

The Army

This chapter will attempt to answer, very summarily, the
following questions: first, how dominant is the role of the
Army? Second, where does the balance of power lie between
the political and military leaders? Who are, and have been,
those military leaders and what has been their background
and training? What has been the pattern of development of
the armed forces? Who are the Army's officers? What sort
of people are its men and women? The response to these
questions will go some way to explaining how, despite recurrent wars and a perpetual state of alert, Israel has profoundly
failed to become a military state. Of course, the position of
the Army and its role in Israel cannot be divorced from
Israeli attitudes to the Arabs, both within and outside her
frontiers; but this will be looked at in more detail in a later
chapter.

Soldiering was the last thing associated with diaspora
Jewry. It was in response to force of circumstances that
early settlers organised their own community defence forces,
HaShomer (the Guards) and the Haganah (the Defence
Force). These precursors were touched upon in chapter 1.
Their influence on the Israeli Defence Force was funda-
mental, and goes far to explain the differences between the
IDF and the armies of other Western liberal democracies.
The key factor is that the Haganah was essentially a part-
time citizens' defence force. It had no historical traditions

of national glory, ceremonial uniforms, parades, or a conventional hierarchy and discipline.

'The Israeli Army', wrote Yigal Allon, 'was made in action – it was a national liberation army.' He may well have seen it that way, for he was one of its young generals in 1949. By that time the British Mandate had degenerated into a military occupation, holding down a situation wherein Jews were fighting off Arabs, and an extreme faction of them actively opposing the British occupiers. On Independence Day, 15 May 1948, the deadline for the British withdrawal, full-scale war was already being waged in several parts of the country. With such turbulent beginnings, followed by persistent threats of annihilation from all her neighbours, it is, on the face of it, remarkable that Israel became, from birth, a vigorous democracy and not a military dictatorship.

Anyone who had followed her history, even so far, would have known better. Once the new state had established frontiers to her territory, there was never the slightest question about the legitimacy of David Ben Gurion as civilian head of government, nor about his first major stroke of domestic policy, which was the assimilation of all the armed forces into the new IDF and the subordination of the military high command to the civilian government. This happened without serious incident, but only as a conscious act of political will. The people of Israel wholeheartedly supported Ben Gurion in this statement about the type of society they wanted.

In fact, in 1949, the existing High Command of the Haganah simply became the High Command of the IDF. The best of the Palmach spirit was preserved and propagated, but the first generation of generals were wise enough to realise that allegiance to the new state must be undivided. It was not only, or even chiefly, over the Palmach that Ben Gurion needed to assert his authority. Israel had no room for terrorist groups like Etzel and Lech'i who had continued to operate outside the authority of the Haganah. The Altalena incident became symbolic of Ben Gurion's determination to break the terrorists. The cargo ship Altalena was unloading arms for Etzel off Haifa in May 1948. Ben Gurion ordered it to stop. It refused, and Ben Gurion then ordered it to be fired upon by the IDF. It burst into flames and twelve of its crew were killed. The symbolic value of a Jewish army firing on Jews was perhaps magnified at the time, but politics operates largely through symbolic acts. Ben Gurion had made his intention clear to create a unified state under a unified command.

On the civilian side, there was no Defence Department in the Jewish Shadow administration in Palestine until the 1940s. Ben Gurion decided against calling it the Ministry of Defence, using the Hebrew word 'Haganah', but instead chose the word 'Bitahon', meaning security. It was another of his symbolic gestures. To this day that is the Hebrew title of what is commonly translated as Defence Ministry. The growth of an autonomous power base in what we, following custom, will call the Defence Establishment, has been a crucial factor in the balance in civilian-military relations. Ben Gurion, aware of this, kept the Defence portfolio in his own hands, and for fourteen of the first fifteen years of the state's existence he was both Prime Minister and Defence Minister. The Defence Establishment flourished in the capable hands of first Eshkol and then Peres, both still civil servants, while political responsibility and active policy-direction remained with the Prime Minister right up to the eve of the 1967 war. Peres became the technocrat, the *bitzuist*, the man who made things happen in the Defence Department. He was in no way an Army man. His near contemporary, Dayan, on the other hand, was essentially a soldier and did not hesitate to knock on political doors to further his military ideas.

Perhaps it is always a more delicate matter for a right-wing government to keep a tight rein on its military chiefs. Begin does not seem to have been so keenly aware of the problem as his predecessors, and General Sharon made no secret of his ambition to be Defence Minister. There were other factors in the equation in 1982, but Sharon's over-zealous military activities in Lebanon confirmed many peoples' forebodings. We shall return to Sharon later in this chapter.

Shimon Peres is quite specific about the formal division of responsibility. 'The Chief of Staff and the Ministry are responsible to the Minister of Defence. Broadly speaking everything appertaining to men materials and equipment until they reach and after they leave the Army, is the responsibility of the Ministry of Defence. Once they are in the Army they are under the Army's authority. The military staff is thus engaged in the organisation and command of the forces, training, intelligence and operations and the maintenance of all personnel except for the top-ranking officers. The civilian arm is concerned with control, finances, the acquisition, production and development of arms and equipment, and the maintenance of senior officers. Peres himself was largely concerned with procurement, and so large a slice of national resources, in money and manpower, has had to be diverted to the acquisition, production and development of arms and equipment over the years that the national economy has developed a permanent limp, and the Defence Department has become a pacemaker for whole sectors of the Israeli economy. This aspect of the matter will be examined in a later chapter.

In 1956 the Sinai War broke out. With the tacit blessing of Britain and France, Israel struck south through the Sinai Desert towards Egypt and crossed the Suez Canal. Using an Israeli attack as a prelude to dethroning Nasser was a shrewd move on the part of Britain and France, since they could then 'intervene' to force the Israelis and the Egyptians to withdraw from both banks of the Canal.

Israel had seen the Suez crisis coming and made strenuous efforts to equip herself for it. The closing of the Suez Canal itself meant nothing to Israel. The blockading of the Gulf of Aqaba meant more, since her oil supplies from Iran came in that way to Eilat. But the crux of the matter was that in 1955, a year after the official British withdrawal from the Canal Zone, Egypt and Syria had both signed arms pacts with the Soviet Union. Nasser was making a serious bid for leadership of the Arab world, and Israel saw herself as an obvious focus of hostility whose destruction could consolidate Egypt's military hegemony and prestige in the area. Israel knew America had not yet decided whether she was a pawn worth queening in the geo-political chess-game, so she did not expect help from Washington. Both Britain and France on the other hand had reasons for wishing to see Nasser deflated and removed from the world scene, without themselves openly courting reproach from their Arab diplomatic friends. Israel felt she could handle the situation. A secret treaty was signed at Sèvres, just outside Paris, between Britain, France and Israel, and Israel subsequently launched the first pre-emptive strike of the Suez Campaign. It was a spectacular success. The world woke up to Israel's existence. General Dayan became a legend overnight, although it was by no means a one-man show and Israel's success was attributable to a whole cadre of intelligent and imaginative commanders and also to a visceral will for national survival. Nasser was humiliated, and indignant American pressure forced a withdrawal by Israeli forces to 1949 borders. But an important change had occurred. The United States began to regard the maverick state of Israel as a serious potential ally in an area they saw turning politically to the Eastern bloc. But, as everyone said at the time, the Sinai Campaign granted Israel time, not peace.

The time Israel won in 1956 ran out in 1967. By this time the IDF had been forged into an efficient fighting force with some 800 tanks and 300 combat aircraft, and a total reserve strength of about 264,000 troops. But this time the Egyptians acted in concert with the other Arab states. They moved in across the Sinai and the small United Nations force there withdrew meekly from their path. Eshkol and his cabinet agonised for weeks over whether to launch a pre-emptive strike against the Egyptians. Eventually they did strike before Egyptians troops actually reached Israeli soil: they bombed Egyptian air-bases to prevent air raids on Tel Aviv and other Israeli towns. Jordan and Iraq moved into the area on the west bank of the river Jordan, Syria and Iraq attacked the Golan Heights north-east of Galilee, and Saudi Arabia lent backing to the Jordanians. The Arab forces mustered double the men and triple the tanks and aircraft of the Israelis.

Israel won. First they drove the Syrians back up the Golan Heights until their forces overlooked Damascus, instead of Syrian troops overlooking Galilee. Then they pushed the Jordanians back across the Jordan River and the Egyptians back across the Suez Canal. This was the Six-Day War. Israel lost 766 men. The Arabs never announced their casualties. This time Israel remained in the territories she had occupied. The occupation of the Golan and the West Bank was strategically vital at that time, but the Sinai was not crucial to Israel's security, and Palestinian guerilla activity never ceased in the Israeli-occupied Gaza strip where thousands of Palestinian refugees had been living since 1949.

From the close of the Six-Day War to Nasser's death in 1970, open warfare was abandoned in favour of active harassment of Israeli positions along the Suez Canal. This forced the Israeli General Staff to keep a large number of men on alert and the resulting drain on manpower was damaging to the economy of such a small country. This campaign was stepped up in 1969 and became known as the War of Attrition. In fact, far from forcing Israel to reconsider her frontiers, it only stiffened her resolve and provoked retaliatory raids deep into Egyptian territory. When Nasser died the War of Attrition was abandoned, but one interesting legacy was the need felt by his successor, Anwar el-Sadat,

57

for an Egyptian anti-aircraft missile defence system. It is a well-known fact that by 1973 Russian anti-aircraft missiles had been installed all along the Canal and around Cairo, and were responsible for heavy Israeli casualties.

So events limped on to the Yom Kippur War of October 1973. This time Israel was caught by surprise on the highest religious holiday of the Jewish year, and great were the recriminations about who was to blame for that failure of Israel's Intelligence estimate. It was her closest brush with defeat. 'We will win because we must win,' said Golda Meir. 'Our neighbours are fighting not for their lives, not for their sovereignty, they are fighting to destroy us. We will not be destroyed. We dare not be destroyed.' Certainly Arab proclamations from all sides did testify to a quite fanatical determination to wipe Israel off the map. After heavy casualties Israel rallied, and with 2,300 dead she was left holding her pre-October 1973 frontiers, with the exception of a UN buffer-zone east of Suez.

The diplomatic initiative which prompted President Sadat to visit Jerusalem in 1977, and the protracted peace negotiations which ensued, are discussed elsewhere in their foreign relations context. Meanwhile terrorist attacks against Israeli settlements in the north continued across the Lebanese border.

Since the mid nineteenth century Lebanon had been regarded as the 'Switzerland of the Middle East', mainly on account of its political stability in a particularly volatile area and its reputation as a financial centre. The Lebanese political system was confessional, in the sense that political representation in national affairs was directly related to religious affiliation. By convention, the President of Lebanon was always a Maronite Christian, the Prime Minister a Sunni Muslim, and the Speaker of the House of Representatives a Shia Muslim. In this way the balance of power was maintained. The President was always Christian because in the 1860s, when the system was established by the French, the

Maronites were numerically the largest group in the country, followed by the Sunni Muslims and then the Shia Muslims and smaller sects.

The longstanding French connection deserves a brief historical mention here. Since 1839 the French had, through capitulatory privileges, undertaken the protection of the Maronite and Catholic minorities in that part of the Ottoman Empire, just as the British had similarly undertaken the protection of the Jewish minority in the area. A sizeable Christian community had grown up in the Sanjak of Lebanon, and when the French laid the legal foundations of the state they deliberately drew its frontiers so as to embrace this Christian community and exclude certain predominantly Muslim areas in the region. The Mandates Commission had the same object in mind when it defined the territories of the French and British Mandates. The Christians had long enjoyed close relations with international banking and financial circles and the French connection reinforced their predominance.

In 1975 civil war broke out in Lebanon over two issues: first, the demographic balance had changed over the years in favour of the Sunni Muslims, who consequently felt they were undeservedly kept in second place in a state headed by a Christian President. Second, there had been a large influx of Palestinians from Jordan after their expulsion by King Hussein in 1970, and this further altered the balance in favour of the Muslims. This imbalance finally gave rise to armed bands of militias: Phalangists, left-wing Muslim groups and Palestinians. After 1970 the Palestinians consolidated their position in the south of Lebanon and in certain enclaves further north. The situation festered. The Christian President, conscious that he held the ultimate sanction of armed force, was not inclined to yield. The demographic balance had tipped against him and short of redefining the national frontiers there was no way the Christians were going to be able to retain their dominant political, economic and

59

military position. After the Black September expulsion of Palestinians from Jordan the drift to civil war seemed unstoppable. For three years the country was battered and drained by full-scale civil war.

Beirut, the national capital, was partitioned into two sectors, Christian and Muslim, with the predominantly commercial heart of the city in the hands of the Christians. The rest of the country fell into a pattern of sectarian fiefdoms. When the civil war officially ended the newly elected Christian President Sarkis tried to reassert his legitimacy over the rival bands of militias who, in effect, controlled the country, but he found this beyond his capability, lacking as he did the firm allegiance of a national army. The Palestinians did their utmost to destabilise Sarkis' fragile authority. The Syrians seconded the Palestinians in this respect, but their more positive aim was to support the Muslim element in Lebanon and prevent the establishment of a dominant Christian régime there. The Israelis would have liked to see Sarkis take firm control so that they would at least have someone with whom to carry on a peaceful dialogue across their northern border, but it became clear that Sarkis had neither the arms, the men nor the real political will to take a grip on his fragmented country, and especially on the Palestinian state within a state in the southern region.

Israel anxiously watched events in Lebanon; especially when her coast and northern settlements became targets of terrorist attacks across the northern border. It had never been a satisfactory or secure frontier from Israel's point of view. Even before the Sykes-Picot Mandate Agreement the World Zionist Congress had expressed the hope of seeing a Jewish homeland that would extend up to the Litani River. But the French, as we have pointed out, had other criteria, and were aware of the number of Christians in that southern sector. For Israel it was a problem that would not go away. In 1948 Ben Gurion, writing in his diary, envisaged 'a Chris-

60

tian state to be set up there with its southern frontier on the Litani'. In 1955 Sharett, Foreign Minister until 1956 and by no means a hard-liner as regards Israel's policies towards her neighbours, quotes a discussion he had on the matter in 1955 with Dayan: 'According to Dayan the only thing that is needed is to find a Lebanese officer, even a major will do. We should either win his heart or buy him with money and get him to agree to declare himself saviour of the Maronite population. Then the Israelis will enter Lebanon, occupy the necessary territory, and set up a Christian régime which will ally itself with Israel. The territory south of the Litani will be annexed to Israel.' Sharett concluded: 'Dayan recommends it be done immediately – tomorrow.'

In 1978 Israel launched Operation Litani. Its objectives were limited, but for various reasons it did not achieve its explicit purpose. For one thing, casualties were relatively high and public opinion was still very conscious of the heavy losses in the Yom Kippur War only five years before. There was agreement that something should be done to stop terrorist attacks from Lebanon, but many people perceived a radical distinction between a war for national survival and one with more limited objectives, however useful and desirable. On a different level the operation clearly made complications for Sadat, who was faced with fierce domestic criticism for entering into a peace agreement with such an 'aggressor against another part of the Arab World'. The Americans had Sadat's interests at heart, as well as their own oil-based diplomacy, when they put strong pressure on Israel to abandon Operation Litani.

It became evident that the Palestinians were going to be a long-term destabilising force in Lebanon, and with the emergence of Yasser Arafat as their international figurehead some sections of the Israeli Army and Defence Establishment became convinced of the urgent need to break the PLO as a military organisation before they were perhaps compelled to open diplomatic negotiations with it. It was

61

with this object in mind that in 1982 Defence Minister Sharon launched his Operation Peace for Galilee. Subsequent events would indicate that this title was, to say the least, something of a misnomer. The immediate objective was to clear a 45-kilometre border strip so that missiles could no longer be launched against towns in northern Galilee. The operation produced a situation where, by the time Israeli troops were scheduled to reach the 45-kilometre line, they were in fact on the outskirts of Beirut. *En route* they found huge quantities of Soviet arms stockpiled underground for use against Israel at some future date.

The Americans, who had given their blessing to the original limited operation, felt Israel was guilty of hubris. Sharon, Minister of Defence and Field Commander in one, possessed neither the innate wisdom nor the temperament to listen to wise advice, and lost his grip on political realities. Whether he had planned to occupy Beirut from the start or had been led on by events remained unclear. In any case this question was swamped by the massive publicity given to one horrific incident in the war. In the course of mopping-up operations Christian Phalangist troops, shortly after the assassination by Muslims of their leader Bashir Gemayel, perpetrated a gruesome massacre of men, women and children in Chatilla and Sabra, two of the PLO camps on the outskirts of Beirut. Although it was established that no Israeli soldiers actually took part in the massacres, they had certainly agreed to Phalangists entering the camps and flushing out terrorists who had taken refuge there. It was never suggested that bands of prisoners would be marched out of the camps. On the other hand neither was it envisaged that the Phalangists would murder women and children in the process. The indictment of the Israeli military command rested on the premise that they should have foreseen the nature of the massacre and taken more positive steps to stop it sooner than they did.

The Chatilla and Sabra incidents were a catalyst. Weeks

62

before the massacres America had led a chorus of protest against an Israeli occupation of Beirut. Arafat canvassed feverishly, and with apparent success, on behalf of the beleaguered PLO. The entire Arab World supported him, because the PLO was one of their best weapons against Israel and indirectly against Israel's protector, America. For a time it looked as if the Americans, the Israeli opposition parties and a section of the Israeli public were, each for their own reasons, determined to put paid to Sharon, and if possible to Begin's Likud government at the same stroke. The United States administration felt he had abused their tacit support for a more limited military action. The Israeli opposition parties saw in him an example of successful military domination of the civilian government – a situation they had always felt should be avoided at all costs. Some sections of the Israeli public felt Sharon's high-handed action and bland self-justification had tarnished Israel's image abroad and diminished her moral standing in the world's eyes. Begin was prevailed upon to set up a Public Enquiry whose report, weeks later, was a model for any country in the circumstances: just, humane and unblinking. It laid moral blame on several high-ranking soldiers and politicians, right up to the head of government, and recommended that Sharon should cease to be Minister of Defence. The Enquiry served several purposes. It quelled a nascent wave of slightly hysterical anti-Israeli feeling in the world press and news media; it appeased a dismayed section of public opinion at home; and it gave Begin time. He could legitimately decide to remain in office until after the Enquiry's report, and by that time moral indignation had cooled and a strong ground-swell of right-wing grass-roots support made itself heard. None of his critics relished the prospect of Begin, or his successor, going to the polls and having Likud returned to power with an increased majority.

What was different about the war in Lebanon from previous Israeli wars? First and foremost that it was not a war for national survival. Soldiers in the Army felt this and so did their families. In Israel there is plenty of feedback at all levels, with a constant traffic of men returning to their families on short leave or when they have served their term. A deep malaise pervaded Israel even before Chatilla. Afterwards the public merely became confused and dismayed by an international whipping which had very little to do with the military situation and everything to do with American and European postures towards Arab states. The Labour opposition did their best to exploit the situation, but it went deeper than party politics. Politicians on all sides were made freshly aware of an old problem: political control of the Army.

So much for the wars. What of the men? Whether admired or deplored it is generally acknowledged that the IDF has a style all its own. It owes very little to the experience of the Jewish Brigade which fought with the British Army in the Second World War. The main British contribution came indirectly through Orde Wingate, who, in his Special Night Squads, set the mark of his very personal style of leadership on every man who served with him. It owes a very great deal to the fighting spirit of the Haganah and of the Palmach, those special operations units set up inside the Haganah by Itzhak Sadeh. Sadeh personally picked and trained Israel's most illustrious future officers, among them Generals Allon, Dayan, Bar Lev and Rabin. Palmach veterans dominated the IDF's senior command between 1953 and 1973. Nearly all from kibbutz or moshav origins, they leaned ideologically to the left, which placed them in sympathy with the governments of that period.

The Labour movement was in two minds about the Army. On the one hand there was Golda Meir's 'No one will make peace with a weak Israel', and that was the gut feeling of most Israelis. On the other hand Ben Gurion was continually reminding them that war should never be an expedient.

War was not to win prizes. Victory was not a prize. Perhaps the national mood is best caught by Rabin, who was a young officer in the thick of the battle for Jerusalem in 1948. He says he and his fellow officers felt they had a moral responsibility to dedicate their lives to ensuring that the state of Israel would never again be unprepared to meet aggression. 'I stayed in the Army,' he says, 'and together with my comrades in arms I fulfilled my pledge to the heroes of the War of Independence. We built a mighty Army.' There was never a Chief of Staff with more human awareness than Rabin. At the high point of his military career, after the ultimate triumphant victory of the 1967 war, Rabin made an extraordinary and moving speech which again testifies to a spirit of deeply reluctant militarism seeking atonement, which is recognisably Israeli. 'The elation of victory had seized the whole nation. Yet among the soldiers themselves a curious phenomenon is to be observed. They cannot rejoice whole-heartedly. Their triumph is marred by grief and shock, and there are some who cannot rejoice at all. The men in the front lines saw with their own eyes not only the glory of victory but also its cost, their comrades fallen beside them soaked in blood. And I know that the terrible price the enemy paid also deeply moved many of our men. Is it because neither their teaching nor their experience has ever habituated the Jewish people to exult in conquest and victory that they receive them with such mixed feelings?'

General Yigal Allon, at the height of his popularity in 1949, was less introspective. He resigned from the Army in 1950 after Ben Gurion disbanded the Palmach, and returned to public life as a Labour politician in 1954; but significantly he was never Minister of Defence. In that first war Israel coined the phrase 'Ain brerah' – 'there is no alternative' – long before Mrs Thatcher adopted it in a debased context. Allon's definition has the 'brutal vision' of the Palmach generation. 'Either you win the war or you will be driven into the Mediterranean; you, individually, along with the

65

whole nation.' Having served from the age of eighteen to twenty-seven in the Haganah, he spent the next five years at universities in Israel and England before entering the Knesset. He was less complex than Rabin and more solid than Dayan. He epitomised all that was positive, practical, realistic and hard-headed in the new Israeli. They called themselves 'sabras', the name of a desert fruit with a soft centre and a prickly outside. 'A native-born Israeli', said Robert Graves, 'is the toughest and most vital human being I have come across anywhere.' They were not refugees; they had been born and bred in the land; they had a strong pioneering sense of having made their lives from very little and they felt they owed no one anything. There was an exhilarating moral freedom in fighting all-out for survival. A whole generation of Israelis born between 1910 and 1930 could identify to some extent with Allon.

After the Suez Campaign in 1956 and even more after the spectacular Six-Day War of 1967, the popular hero was Moshe Dayan. With his natural panache, his piratical eye-patch, his easy cameraderie and his sheer physical courage, he became the national and international symbol of Israel's military prowess. But, superb Field Commander as he was, Dayan lacked either the ideological commitment of Allon or the humanistic integrity of Rabin. In the crisis days at the end of May 1967, Eshkol, under pressure, made Dayan Defence Minister, and he remained in that post throughout the triumph of the Six-Day War, its aftermath and on to the end of the near disaster of the Yom Kippur War in 1973. Those years trace the curve of his success. Dayan, the ebullient and charismatic field commander, swept to victory in 1967 with an army meticulously trained under Rabin. Thereafter Dayan, who had eagerly accepted the Defence portfolio so that there would be fewer restraints on his actions as field commander, lacked the stomach for administration. Sachar points out that the civilian command of the armed forces had been cut off from direct involvement in national security issues ever since Dayan's appointment as Minister. His prestige was such that the Cabinet and Knesset made no attempt to control or even understand military thought and policies. Yet in the following year Dayan devoted most of his time to the administration of the occupied territories and paid little attention to the actual state of the Defence infrastructure. Matters of 'housekeeping' bored him.

In his survey of Israel's early Chiefs of Staff, Peres, who worked with them all from his power base in the Defence Ministry, awards Dayan marks only for 'the art of original warfare'. It is to Yadin, who became Chief of Staff in 1950 at the age of thirty-two, that the IDF owes its legal and organisational framework, including the reserve system. Maklef, next in line, consolidated its sound economic management. Laskoff, who succeeded Dayan in 1957, developed co-operation between the three armed forces and tightened discipline. Zvi-Zur introduced the Army to the new weaponry it was receiving by the 1960s from abroad and also beginning to make at home. Lastly, in Peres' list, Rabin, the methodical administrator, trained it to fresh heights of technical efficiency at all levels.

The IDF prides itself on its technical efficiency; and nowhere more than in the Airforce. Its first commander was ex-RAF pilot Ezer Weizmann, who took it in hand in 1958 when the American planes began to arrive. In 1967 it more or less decided the outcome of the war on the first day when it knocked almost the entire Egyptian Airforce. By the mid-1970s the Israeli Aircraft Industry was producing its own Kfir (lion) fighter-bombers and Israeli pilots had earned a reputation for using their own hardware with outstanding technical skill and an economical sense of their cost to a country the size of Israel.

The emphasis on youth in the officer corps of the IDF has been firmly maintained. This means that officers take an active part in training exercises and are capable of perpetuating the principles of Wingate and Dayan that they should personally lead into battle. The fact that Israel's casualty lists always contain such a high proportion of officers speaks for itself.

It has been both inevitable and intentional that the Army should have been a predominant force in unifying the nation. Every man does three years national service from the age of eighteen to twenty-one, and nearly all women do two and a half years. Thereafter the men are in the reserve until the age of forty-five and train for two months each year with their units. This is the only way such a small country can keep a trained force and continue her economic development. The regular Army is very small, so that the reserves' training is no mere formality; reservists serve in all branches of the service, including parachute, submarine, flying and tank-crew operations, while promising recruits are sent with minimum delay for officer training. The atmosphere is informal. It has been noted that there is no word in Hebrew for the ritual 'sir', even in the Army; no separate messes, Christian names all round and a minimum of saluting and square-bashing. Perhaps Peres has the answer: 'The IDF', he says, 'rejects the motion that you have to 'break' a civilian before you can make a soldier of him. We believe you have to build up the civilian to turn him into a fighting civilian.'

In 1948 women fought and died in the front lines. But then the front line was everywhere and the Army had only the most elementary weapons. Today the women do most of the clerical work, and, apart from nursing, are trained to handle the increasingly sophisticated electronic communications network. A growing number of instructors are women, at all levels, the assumption being that no man wants to strip and reassemble his weapons or locate a fault in his tank engine more slowly than his girl-instructor. The women's natural teaching skills are also used in the more conventional classroom, consolidating the Hebrew and possibly the general education of new immigrants; also working in the schools and adult education centres in new settlements, most of which, in recent years, have been set up in the less hospitable parts of the country. The Army has been the melting-pot of sabras and immigrants, of Eastern and Western traditions. After a nine-months' crash course in Hebrew and three years national service, the immigrant is recognisably Israeli.

Because Israeli soldiers are fighting civilians, and because they are not depersonalised in training, they remain human beings; they keep their eyes open and do not treat military service as just a slice cut out of their lives when they suspend all judgement. Soldiers on short leave are known to attend public demonstrations concerning the war they are fighting. They talk gravely in public, in the ordinary bus taking them to or from their unit, about the morality of their own actions and those of the government. It is hard to escape the conviction that the Israeli people as a whole are profoundly unmilitaristic.

That said, there are, of course, exceptions. Old-fashioned right wing Zionism has never been afraid to recommend the sword to assist the designs of the Almighty. Ben Gurion quenched that fire in the 1950s, but it has not ceased to smoulder, and to its discredit a right-wing Zionist government has not shrunk from fanning its embers. Middle-aged Israelis and many of their children will point on their television screens to a new proletariat of Eastern Jews in the cities and the new towns, enraptured by Begin's rhetoric, clamouring ritually for 'Begin, Melek Israel' (Begin, King of Israel), and they will murmur darkly of the spectre of fascism, or even of Levantinisation. They deplore what they call macho imagery and aggressive nationalism. Perhaps if they could afford to travel abroad they would see their angry crowds in better perspective. Yet they are right to be worried. Their more complicated uneasiness about how to live without aggression with the Arabs within their frontiers will be discussed in a later chapter.

69

4

Religion

Israel is a Jewish state. Every Jew who settles in Israel has an automatic right to Israeli citizenship. But one has to understand that to be Jewish is not the equivalent of being Catholic or Church of England. It is both more and less. So, too, the Jewish nature of the state of Israel is something different from the Englishness of England or the Frenchness of France. For one thing it is still relatively new; yet linked to a past, and a dream of a past, which is very ancient. Secondly, the state itself is still precarious, in the sense that it lacks the recognition of all but one of its neighbours. It is also the scene of an experiment, wherein Jews from all over the world have become fully social human beings on their own terms. It is perhaps understandable, therefore, that they opted for an integrated Jewish identity. A Jewish state, at least for the first few generations.

What did Jews from Russia or Chicago have in common with Jews from Germany or Argentina, except their religious and social traditions and an attachment to the biblical land of their forefathers? Yet any Jew arriving in that land could not fail to find some reinforcement of his inculcated sense of belonging there. For a religious Jew the experience could be one of exalted self-revelation. For any Jew driven there by persecution because of his Jewishness, it was both a safe-house and a place where he could live freely and openly and still be a Jew. What, these people felt instinctively, had anyone else to do with their Jewish homeland? It was a homeland for Jews, no more, no less. Of course it would be a Jewish state. That was what they had got used to calling it while it was still a dream. Every year at Passover they would repeat the liturgy 'HaShanah haba'ah biYerushalaim' – 'next year in Jerusalem'.

'The Return' would be to Jerusalem, with all its symbolic meaning: site of the first and second Temples and the Wailing Wall, capital of ancient Israel and focus through the centuries of Jewish national sentiment. Not that most of the early settlers would have called themselves religious Jews. Zionism had very little to do with religious orthodoxy. One can trace an interesting path followed by many of the Russian Zionists: first the abandonment of their Orthodox faith to become ardent social and political reformers; then the realisation, especially in Russia, that their Jewishness still set them apart in national politics; so that they transferred their hopes and idealism to Zionism. The Zionist commitment could be said to have filled the role of religion for a generation of people who had lost their inherited faith. This may, incidentally, go some way to explaining the passionate character of Israeli politics.

During the Mandate years the question of religion and the state did not arise. In chapter 1 mention was made of how the millet system left room for the free activity of religious institutions, Muslim, Christian and Jewish alike, at community level. Judaism is, in any case, not given to constitutional hierarchy; it is community-based. Some settlements had a rabbi, others did not. Only in 1948 did the question arise of the new state's relation to what had been communal religious institutions. The Declaration of Independence, in fact, clearly envisages a secular state which is to be 'based on freedom, justice and peace as envisaged by the prophets of Israel . . . and will guarantee freedom of religion, conscience, language and culture'. It does not contain a single direct reference to the Deity.

71

In chapter 1 it was suggested that the Mandatory restrictions provoked the establishment of a comprehensive system of secular self-government under the nominal umbrella of religious bodies, and how, at Independence, those arrangements were, for the sake of continuity in time of war, transferred lock, stock and barrel to the Provisional Government. That was logical enough. What does need explaining, however, is why, after the war, Prime Minister Ben Gurion let that situation continue.

The answer is partly convenience, and partly what Safran calls 'an element of ambivalence in the attitude and thinking of secularly inclined Israelis with respect to the Jewish religion and its relation to their state'. On the negative side, they did not share the Western European historical experience wherein the nation states emerged only by separating themselves from a universal Catholic Church; so they felt no imperative *need* for separation of church and state. On the positive side, they saw in the Jewish faith a key to their Jewish identity. This question of 'What is a Jew?' loomed large in the twenty years after Independence. Israelis sense that community of religion, be it formal, passive, or even merely negative, is the link between them and Jews in the rest of the world.

It was in a somewhat ambiguous frame of mind, therefore, that the founding fathers allowed the Orthodox wing among them to assume extra-ordinary powers in the early years of the state. The key to this power lay in the religious political parties and what Sachar calls 'Israel's bicephalous judiciary': the dual system of civil and rabbinical courts carried over from the Mandate.

On the whole Israel's judicial system was strongly influenced by the British tradition of common law and equity, together with some Ottoman influences, especially concerning land ownership, and also the Biblical and Talmudic sources of Jewish law. After Independence a determined religious minority group insisted that the rabbinical

72

courts were given increased powers. For instance, under the Mandate participation in the Jewish community had been voluntary, but in 1953 an Act of Knesset gave the rabbinical courts extensive authority in matters of personal status (nationality, marriage, divorce, etc) and included under their jurisdiction 'any Jewish national or resident of Israel'. This was, on the face of it, an enormous concession, and it provoked vociferous public protest; but Ben Gurion's Mapai government found it expedient to enter into a political marriage of convenience with the religious parties, because in return they ensured him a stable political base from which he could attend to urgent defence matters. So when, on Saturdays and religious holidays, many public services were stopped, shops, offices and banks closed, and all the Army kitchens were made kosher, Ben Gurion said he felt all this was a small price to pay. But the religious parties soon raised the price of their support; first, financial assistance for religious schools, then exemption from national service for Orthodox girls because of the alleged 'infamy' and 'defilement' it involved. To the non-religious all this appeared as creeping clericalism, and, in its effect on the status of women, as the heedless application of harsh and obsolete laws.

The clerical establishment soon developed formidable political muscle: from the Ministry of Religious Affairs and the Chief Rabbinate to the Rabbinical Council, the religious courts and the local religious councils. There were originally only two Zionist religious parties, the Mizrachi party and the Mizrachi Workers' party; and two non-Zionist parties, the Agudat Israel and the Agudat Israel Workers. The last two were non-Zionist in the religious sense that they questioned the legitimacy of anyone but the Almighty to create a Jewish state. All four groups were firmly in the hands of European Jews. In 1956 the two Mizrachi parties fused to form the National Religious Party (NRP) and managed to rub along with Ben Gurion's socialist Mapai without too much friction; but the two Agudat Israel parties were introverted and fundamentalist, concentrated in Jerusalem, and they teamed up to form the Torah Religious Front. They, too, joined Ben Gurion's Mapai coalition, but only, in Sachar's words, to 'tighten the religionists' grip on the legislative jugular' and share in the spoils. Since 1959 (except for very brief interludes) these two religious blocs have contributed between 15 and 18 Knesset votes in support of every coalition government: socialist until 1977 and Likud after 1977.

Before the formation of every coalition, the leader of the largest group in the Knesset undertakes negotiations with all the smaller groupings which might possibly be partners. The NRP have brought to the coalition table a fairly predictable selection of demands, and the extent to which they have left their mark on law and policy-making has depended on the weakness of the dominant coalition party. Sometimes a policy issue could be traded for a seat in the cabinet, or vice versa. In fact the religious parties have kept almost continuous control over the Departments of the Interior and Religious Affairs, and over the Department of Education and Cultural Affairs. The fact is every Prime Minister so far has felt, when it came to the crunch, that their support was cheap at the price, and for their part the religious parties have usually been discreet enough to confine their intervention to matters concerning their chosen spheres of influence. One result of this has been that left and right do not have discernibly different policies in these fields. The price to the electorate as a whole, in terms of irritation and frustration, has sometimes been disproportionate, but the average Israeli has, until recently, demonstrated an unusually developed appreciation of political realities. There is no doubt that Israel's anachronistic laws governing the family (marriage, divorce, abortion, dietary laws, and even autopsies) are the direct result of pressure from a minority group of religious zealots; but only when the religious cloak is extended to

74

broader national issues like settlements in the occupied territories, public transport or the work schedules of the national airline, El-Al, are the grass roots stirred to protest.

One factor here has been the personality and prestige of Josef Burg, a septuagenarian who has held cabinet posts almost without a break since 1951. He is moderate and a pragmatist, with a warm, down-to-earth sense of humour, and he has to some extent tempered the fervour of some of his NRP colleagues. Zevulun Hammer is Burg's natural potential successor. Although he rose to power on the shoulders of the extremist group Gush Emunim, which tends to hit the headlines whenever Jewish settlements are either established or demolished in occupied territory, he has acquired a measure of pragmatism from Burg, or simply from political experience, and in his hands the NRP is unlikely to see its influence diminished.

A second factor in the strength of the religious parties lies in the way the pattern of their support has been affected by demographic change in the country. In the first four years after the creation of the state, 700,000 immigrants poured into Israel, more than doubling the population. Another 700,000 entered in the fifteen years after that. Half the newcomers came from Muslim countries and most of the other half came from communist Eastern Europe. Socialist idealism meant little to these people, but since all these immigrants acquired the right to vote the moment they landed in the country, the political parties were compelled to appeal to them in terms that were relevant to them, such as national sentiment, charismatic leadership and bread-and-butter issues. The Oriental Jews did not question the religious status quo, accustomed as they had been to a far more restrictive social structure in their Muslim countries of origin. They tended to view the relations between religion and the state in Israel in Muslim terms, except that in Israel Jews rather than Muslims constituted the dominant corporate group. To these people the problem was merely

75

one of how best to make religion more applicable to modern life.

The strength of the religious group is now, if anything, on the increase. When Begin formed his coalition in January 1981 he had 48 seats compared with Labour's 48. By successfully courting the three religious groupings of the day he gained 13 extra seats and a majority of one in the Knesset. Rumour had it that Labour offered Burg the premiership itself if he would desert Begin. Burg stayed and the coalition agreement included Sabbath observance in all government offices, enormous increases in subsidies to religious establishments, no national sporting events on the Sabbath, El-Al grounded on the Sabbath and on religious festivals, and more equipment to be imported by the National Electricity Company to replace human hands on the Sabbath. Yet in 1981 89 per cent of the electorate did *not* vote for religious orthodoxy.

Since the late 1970s a young faction within the NRP has come into prominence: the Gush Emunim (Block of the Faithful). They are not predominantly Oriental Jews and many are of American stock. They have adopted a defiant stand against surrendering any part of Judea and Samaria, the Biblical provinces belonging to the Jews. They have tried to force the hand of the government by establishing unauthorised settlements in the areas in question in order to 'create facts' that would be difficult to dismantle. In 1982 they attracted maximum media-coverage of the government-enforced abandonment of settlements in Sinai, in accordance with the Camp David Agreements, and in general they oppose any compromise solution to the West Bank problem. It is too early to say whether the Gush Emunim are more than a temporary phenomenon. They certainly do no good to Israel's image abroad, and their publicity-seeking tactics are out of tune with the customary low profile kept by the religious parties.

It was interesting to note that Zevulun Hammer, a product

of Gush Emunim, raised one of the loudest voices calling on Begin to set up a full-scale commission of enquiry into the much-publicised Phalangist massacre at Chatilla and Sabra refugee camps in Lebanon. It was good to see that the NRP are consciously guardians of the righteousness of the Jewish state, in major as well as in minor matters. For if one thing became evident in the last weeks of the war in Lebanon in 1982, it was that Israel sets great store by the moral rectitude and humanity of her government and her army, and that Jews, and Gentiles too, the world over, also set special standards for Israel.

Judaism certainly plays a part in every Jew's conscious image of himself, as a Jew; though, paradoxically, not as an Israeli. 'Who needs to be Orthodox when you live in Israel?' some will say. Shimon Peres, leader of the Labour party, says unashamedly, 'I am convinced that Israel is the story of man at his best. This belief is the torch that guides our footsteps and illuminates our paths.' Arrogance or an assumption of daunting moral responsibility?

Israelis have tended to agonise about their place in the world, about their relations with the Arabs, and about the way the world sees them. Far from sweeping unpleasant facts under the carpet they have insisted on purging themselves through public atonement, making themselves a spectacle for a curious international press and a puzzled international public. Israel's image abroad is far from clear. Cameramen are apt to focus on the religious costumes and trappings of the Orthodox and the hora dance-ring, if only because 99 per cent of Israel looks too ordinary and low key to be photogenic. So many Israelis from all walks of life speak some English, or French, or German, that the average journalist is assailed by a confusion of conflicting opinions and stories. He is tempted to fall back on the religious costumes and the hora dancers; or, if he is a war correspondent, on Arabs – preferably Arab women in identifiably Arab clothes. If a film is made about Israeli soldiers, it has more

77

appeal if it is one of the few units that carry prayer shawls and yomulkas. For the outside world Orthodox religion is the cheap media-symbol of Israel.

5

The Economy

'Small countries', said Shimon Peres, 'have to be like Alice's rabbit and run for all they are worth in order to stay in the same place.' Israel is a very small country. She has a population of about 3.5 million Israelis in an area of some 8,000 square miles, together with 700,000 Arabs in the Occupied Territories, and her economic resources are almost exclusively man-made within the last fifty years. Economic progress has been at a phenomenal rate.

In 1982, for the first time since the early 1950s, her GNP failed to grow; imports rose and exports fell creating a serious balance of payments deficit. While private consumption increased and people bought more cars and more consumer durables, real wages fell by 2.5 per cent and inflation was around 130 per cent. Is Israel running more slowly, or is she merely feeling the chill winds of economic change that have been buffeting the rest of the world?

It has always been difficult for Israel to appreciate the crude laws of economics and assess how far her economic survival (we are not here talking of political survival) has been due to financial aid from overseas Jews and the United States Government, and how far to her own unorthodox commercial dynamism. Defence contracts, foreign aid, reparations, and the contributions of the Jewish National Fund are all integral parts of the Israeli economic equation. So, too, are other specifically Israeli phenomena like the kibbutz movement and the Histadrut.

It is easy to overlook the very limited time-scale of Israel's economic development. The Turks, in the three centuries they occupied Palestine, contributed virtually nothing to it. The British, between 1917 and 1948, laid a limited communications infrastructure for their own purposes; roads for military traffic, a deep-water port at Haifa, the outlet of the oil pipeline from the Gulf; a single-track railway linking Haifa with the Damascus-Mecca Railway and another stretch up from Tel Aviv to Jerusalem. The development of Palestine as an economic unit was outside their terms of reference, and out of the question until the demographic issue had been settled. They saw their task as a military holding-operation. Before 1948 Israel was a land of capitalist citrus plantations and impoverished subsistence farmers, with an insecure commercial proletariat in the two ports of Haifa and Jaffa-Tel Aviv.

Economic organisation began, perforce, at the grass roots. As soon as the Jewish settlements progressed beyond the charity of Rothschild and the Jewish National Fund, they set up producers' and consumers' co-operatives: HaPoel HaTzair, Poalei Zion, and after 1917 Achdut HaAvoda. In 1920 these joined a labour federation known as the Histadrut. The majority of the Histadrut's early members belonged to moshavim and kibbutzim and heavy emphasis was placed on creating jobs for Jews on the land. This combined the Zionist ideal of rebuilding the country with the socialist aim of establishing a Jewish workers' society in Palestine. To this day the kibbutzim are the mainstay of Israel's agricultural production, both of food and of raw materials, and many have also diversified into light industry. In the 1920s the Histadrut turned to the needs of urban workers, too, and set up labour exchanges, organised collective bargaining and tried to force Jewish employers to eschew cheap Arab labour and employ Jews. Believing more in example than precept, it set up, in 1923, Hevrat HaOvdim, a holding company for a variety of dependent undertakings: among them, HaMashbir HaMerkazi to buy and market the produce of the kibbutzim and moshavim; Tnuva, for dairy goods; Shikun, a housing company; a workers' bank, the Bank HaPoalim; an insurance company; and the Egged Bus Company. By 1939 the Histadrut was operating some 1,000 enterprises, and its empire continued to expand after independence all the while the Labour government was in power.

Under the Mandate, with the impossibility of any central government machinery, the Histadrut also became the linchpin for a whole range of public services not undertaken by the British administration and neglected by private investors. Solel Boneh built roads, houses and offices, drained swamps, and even, once it was well established, took on contracts from the British. A health fund, the Kupat Holim, had been in existence since 1911, and through it the Histadrut ran its own hospitals and rural health centres. It ran schools (nearly half of all Hebrew schools at one time) and adult education courses; it had its own newspaper, *Davar*, and its own theatre company, Ohel. For a majority of the yishuv the Histadrut was all but synonymous with Jewish Palestine itself. It had always operated at two levels, economic and political, and as the pre-state political parties took shape it was natural that the Histadrut slipped under the control of the workers' party, Mapai, which became the governing party for the first nineteen years of statehood.

For the first five years after independence the country was faced with mass immigration, near bankruptcy and a dearth of private capital, local or foreign, to cope with the situation. The economic infrastructure was woefully underdeveloped and over half the population was packed in reception camps and poor housing in and around Tel Aviv and Haifa. The most urgent need was to disperse them and produce food. In those critical years over half of all

81

government expenditure went on housing, with defence the next highest item, for the Arabs were not accepting Israel's presence quietly. There was neither time nor inclination to reshape the machinery of administration. The Histadrut and the Mapai political leadership were comrades-in-arms. Those were the hardest years, with rationing, insecurity, no foreign aid and only the loyal trickle of support from the JNF.

In 1952 German reparations were a life-giving injection; $820 million to be spread over a twelve-year period, though much of it in German goods. Eshkol launched his New Economic Policy. A Reparations Corporation was set up to channel the money into growth sectors: ports, electricity generation, irrigation, a merchant fleet, the exploitation of minerals in the Negev Desert. It made a breathing space. By the mid 1950s GNP was growing at 8.7 per cent a year. The worst was over.

A short-term headache but a long-term blessing were the 142,000 North African Jews who entered the country in the years 1952 to 1958. Educationally and socially the majority of them belonged to the Third World and came with nothing, not even a serviceable trade. To get them out of the transit camps and avoid their gravitating to urban slums, they were settled in new development towns, many in the Negev, in carefully mixed communities of two-fifths sabras to three-fifths Maghreb immigrants. Towns they have now become, but in the early years they were concrete outposts in the desert. It was an intelligently planned and well-intentioned operation but it could not hope to be 100 per cent successful. A remarkable number of the first generation did take root in that unpromising soil, but today their children are not so appreciative. They resent their parents' hardship and the assumption that European culture constitutes the melting-pot into which, they claim, all other cultural forces are expected to dissolve. On the other hand, European veterans argue that in their day they were never so cosseted with housing, medicine and jobs when they were new immigrants. Things in Israel move fast, and expectations with them. The long-term answer is seen in education, including adult education, together with the assimilating influence of military service, which will, it is hoped, open the doors of opportunity to second-generation Maghreb Jews and reveal to them the superior blessings of Western culture. The 38,000 Iraqi and Yemenite immigrants found less problems in assimilation, either because of their educational background or a less traumatised cultural history.

The economic take-off that started in 1952 had reaped a 250 per cent growth in GNP by 1965. It was based not on the traditional foundations of ample raw materials and cheap labour, but rather on the consumer demand of a burgeoning immigrant population. In the absence of accumulated private wealth, investment had to be orchestrated by the state, and in this task it had the co-operation and experience of the Histadrut behind it. The Histadrut could channel government funds (budgeted or foreign aid) where the government felt they were most needed. It would enlist what private capital (domestic or foreign) was available, and set up a corporation. Sometimes, but not necessarily, the Histadrut would indirectly retain a controlling share interest in the concern. Later KOOR was set up to perform this function for the Histadrut, and it would take a great deal of research to unravel all KOOR's associations. A recent assessment puts its assets at $2.9 billion spread over some 250 companies, including major arms producers like IMI (Israeli Military Industries), SOLTAM and TADIRAN, the latter a joint concern run by KOOR in collaboration with the American electronics company, General Telecommunications and Electronics. The result of all this is that in Israel there exists what Eisenstadt called an 'interesting coalescence' between the public sector and large-scale entrepreneurs in the private sector. From time to time accusations of political corruption are bandied about, but by international standards the offences involve mere chickenfeed. More pertinent are criticisms that the Histadrut empire squeezes out private competition and adopts a complacent attitude to wage inflation. Such criticism need not be taken less seriously just because it is often made in a party political context.

At the head of KOOR today is ex-General Gavish, a hero of the Six-Day War. One should not attach undue importance to the number of ex-generals in the commercial and political élite. With compulsory reserve military service from eighteen to thirty-five, and five wars in thirty-five years, it would reflect poorly on the Army if the country's best managers had not reached the highest rank. There is no evidence of their constituting a common front as a military pressure group. No great private fortunes hang on arms manufacture in Israel. It is, however, a fact that 14 per cent of the workforce is directly engaged in arms production and that Israel needs export markets to support this sector of industry. European arms producers want to supply their own home markets, so Israel has to look to the Third World. In one sense Israel is an attractive proposition for Third World countries, being too small to exert subsequent influence on the use of the goods she supplies. On the other hand many of her potential Third World customers are in the Islamic bloc. Israel proclaims roundly that she will sell to any country who wants to buy on condition that the weapons she sells will not be used against Israel. When you are in the arms business economics is inextricable from foreign relations, and Israel is not alone in perceiving this.

A word must be said here about a totally different sphere of development, and one which also spilled over into foreign relations; the Water Carrier. This was devised as early as 1944 by an American engineer, Lowdermilk, as the answer to the problem that 40 inches of rain fell annually in Galilee but only 1 inch in the Negev. Lowdermilk's plan was to harness the waters of the Jordan before they emptied into the Lake of Galilee and carry them, together with waters from the Yarkon and Kishon Rivers, in an enormous conduit down the entire length of the country, absorbing local water surpluses and purified sewage, and replenishing local shortages *en route*. The Water Carrier runs from Galilee to a point near Beer Sheva. The project inevitably diminished the Jordan waters available to Syria and Jordan, but their objections were overruled. Syrian efforts to dam the sources of the Jordan were flattened by Israeli artillery and planes. The Water Carrier was considered too vital to Israel's development and survival to risk its obstruction. On its completion in 1964 it did, indeed, open up the possibility of Ben Gurion's dream of an Israel supporting 5 million Jews. Three years later 55,000 people were already cultivating 140,000 acres of reclaimed desert in the Negev and the region was self-sufficient in vegetables, fruit and dairy products.

The Negev became 'Israel's future' as Ben Gurion had dreamed it would. But beyond the exercise of making the desert bloom it has also become an industrial region. The old Dead Sea potash works, where the early settlers slaved to dig out their fertiliser, has become a massive complex producing bromine, salt and magnesium chlorides. Methane has been tapped at Zohar and a huge petrochemicals plant built at Arad. There is oil under the desert and copper at Timna in the south near Eilat. And apart from its natural resources the Negev constitutes simply land-space for industries transplanted from elsewhere, once the workforce and infrastructure are in place. The capital of the region is Beer Sheva, which has grown explosively into a desert city, planned deliberately as the administrative, commercial, cultural and military centre. A string of lesser townships has taken shape across the desert: Arad, Kiryat Gat, Dimona, Ashdod, the last as a new port south of Ashkelon for exporting Negev produce. All are models of town-planning, but it will take some years for their trees and parks to mature. The fact is that if Israel is to support her existing population, let alone the immigrants she still hopes to attract, and give them the standard of living they have come to expect, then she must develop new industries, use the skills created by her education system, and keep the national adrenalin flowing with the excitement of something other than war.

In 1967, after the Six-Day War, Israel could afford to think about something other than mere survival. Work-hardened pioneers started to complain about 'the problem of affluence'. Freed from the nagging compulsion of working for survival, the second generation became critical of the quality of the society they had created. 40 per cent of the national income, they complained, was earned (earned, not owned) by 5 per cent of the population, while the bottom 20 per cent earned only 5 per cent of the national income. Comparisons with European countries where the polarisation of wealth is infinitely greater left them unmoved. Labour costs, they said, were rising faster then productivity, and this was all the fault of the Histadrut which blocked wage-freezes and redundancies, froze out private enterprise and exercised a near monopoly on public works contracts. The symbiotic relationship between the Histadrut empire and the political parties, and not only the parties of the left, undoubtedly opened the door to a certain amount of wheeling and dealing. The old idealism was a lamented casualty of Israel's comparative affluence. The European Jews complained of Levantinisation, the Oriental Jews of discrimination. Not until the early 1970s did they become really self-conscious about the Palestinian Arabs.

The Palestinian Arabs have always been a political problem, inside and outside the country. But for many years the Israelis were short-sighted enough to believe that economic prosperity and education would be the solution to the Arab presence inside the country. Not counting the Occupied Territories of Gaza and the West Bank, most Arabs live in villages along the Carmel range inland from Haifa and in

86

towns in that region like Nazareth. They were given the vote, but there are only three Arab members of the Knesset and it is understood that they chiefly concern themselves with Arab affairs. In 1959 the Histadrut gave them full membership. Yet until 1966 there were restrictions on Arab movement inside the country and to the present day the bulk of the Arab population is isolated from Israeli society at large. Only the Druze serve in the Army, for obvious, though not insurmountable reasons, yet this in itself rules out a very powerful force towards social integration. Today, the wisdom acquired through dealing with Oriental Jewish immigrants, who, on arrival, shared many of the deprivations of the Palestinian Arabs, has promoted greater understanding of the Arab minority, and although Israelis may tend to be pushy and uncompromising, at least the colonial attitude of condescension is totally alien to them. Thus, in so far as the Arab population *is* an economic problem, continued progress is likely to be made on that front.

'The cost of security is not a function of the size of the national economy, but of the scale of the hostility surrounding the state.' Shimon Peres was the technocrat most intimately concerned with the demands on Israel's economy of the Defence Department in the first twelve critical years after independence. His contention was that defence spending did not have to be subtracted from the creation of positive wealth; that the acquired skills and technical spin-off could be invaluable to general industrial development; and that defence contracts could stimulate economic self-sufficiency in a variety of fields. There is no denying that the defence budget was crucial to Israel's physical survival in those years. It was not just a question of national pride and flag-waving. There was no alternative, as her leaders never tired of saying. But it is also a fact that the scale of funds allotted to the Defence Department, the guardian of national survival, for a whole range of far-sighted projects, would not have been politically forthcoming had they been requested under a different heading. It was thus that Israel built up an aircraft industry, civil as well as military, despite protests that this was a club reserved for the big nations; a microelectronics industry, extending way beyond its original military purposes; an optical industry which is at the international forefront of work on fibre optics and lasers; and a nuclear programme with a reactor at Dimona which gave rise to some far-fetched and probably well-founded speculation. And all this as one politician put it, while eggs were rationed to one a week.

In the key years of the late 1950s and '60s Israel was fortunate in having Professor Ernst Bergmann as scientific adviser to the Defence Ministry. A pupil of Einstein, he was a man of rare vision and creativity. 'The world', he said, 'is opening up before our generation . . . We must try to harness potential in its earliest stages, even in areas with which we are unfamiliar, so that we can be among the progressive and not the backward nations of our time.' Brave words. It has been argued that Israel could, like Japan, have avoided the expense of her own research by relying on richer countries. Bergmann had an answer to that: 'If there are no experts trained in a field, there is no authority qualified to decide what should be bought and how to exploit the purchased knowledge. Moreoever, a state which sells knowledge is not likely to sell new knowledge that it has not yet exploited itself. The only knowledge that it would be prepared to sell us would be obsolete knowledge of no value.' It is a great thing to live in a country without entrenched economic interests. They will grow in Israel, but for the generation of the 1960s the field was refreshingly open.

Bergmann insisted Israel must and could achieve independence in four vital areas of existence: water, food, arms and energy. Food and water went together to some extent, and were jointly solved for the time being by the Water Carrier and the kibbutz movement. Arms was a question of foreign

88

aid and KOOR. Energy was Israel's Achilles' heel, and solutions needed to be unconventional. Nuclear power was Bergmann's preferred solution. Solar power is now widely used for domestic water-heating. Oil is brought expensively by pipeline up through Eilat. The latest grand design is the Med-Dead Canal, a project of Tennessee Valley proportions which would carry water from the Mediterranean down to the southern tip of the depleted Dead Sea, 400 metres below sea-level. Apart from irrigating the northern Negev on its way (and salt water is only a relative problem now to Israeli farmers), the canal would provide cooling water for a chain of power stations and for the extraction of shale oil which requires vast quantities of water. It is no more fantastic than the Water Carrier. The Bergmann spirit lives on. And it does not need the Defence Department to justify it. The intention is to finance it through a special international issue of Israeli state bonds.

Critics at home have accused Israel of living in a never-never land, floating precariously on American aid. Anxiously she must await the annual sum voted by Congress. For 1983 the figure is $2,485 billion, only a disappointing percentage up on 1982. The reciprocal pressures of the Jewish lobby in American politics and of the State Department on Israeli foreign policy are overt but still incalculable. Much of the American aid is tied to military supply contracts. If Israel could only reduce her military spending, say her home critics, and find some viable *modus vivendi* with her neighbours, she would, at a stroke, be freed from an intolerable drain on her resources and stand in less urgent need of the foreign aid that comes with strings attached. There are even those religious doves who argue that Israel should be prepared to envisage life without foreign aid. This, they say, would force her to live within her means. As long as others pay for our relative affluence (so the argument goes) the Treasury and the nation can defy economic logic. Mr Aridor, the Finance Minister, is accused of placing Israel in the same league as Mexico and Argentina. Does he consider that the deeper the debt the better off the debtor because the international banking system cannot afford to have national governments default?

Israel has always resolutely classed herself with the developed nations. The Third World label was resisted even in the hard-fought 1950s and '60s. On the other hand, economic independence is a gesture she is in no position to make at the present juncture. Nor would it, in all probability, lessen the pressures. She cannot change her geographical position on the most volatile frontier of East and West.

Compared with other Middle Eastern countries Israel is a parliamentary democracy with highly developed political, judicial and commercial institutions and a literate and predominantly highly skilled population living under the umbrella of a welfare state. Income per head is at least five times that found in neighbouring countries and life expectancy is over seventy if one does not count the risks of war.

Compared with Western European countries Israel is still under-industrialised, even though she leads the world in certain limited fields. Her society is relatively classless, the highest salary being only five times the lowest, the life-style of the political and even the commercial élite is relatively modest and unemployment is practically stationary at 2.5 per cent of the adult population. To cope with unparalleled rates of inflation the Histadrut has evolved a system whereby it negotiates a national cost of living allowance, adjusted monthly or quarterly, with the private sector, and a similar agreement with the public sector. This year the Labour-controlled Histadrut was accused of not co-operating with the Treasury over the public-sector allowance, but despite the polarisation of Government and Opposition in the past year the machinery works, by and large.

A word must be said about the Tel Aviv stock exchange, which is unique in the breadth of its clientele. Investors do not need a broker; anyone can buy and sell shares through their bank with a minimum of formalities, and a high proportion of ordinary wage-earners play the market. They do so to supplement their incomes, or as a hedge against inflation, or simply as an outlet for traditional business instinct, and in the relative absence of football pools, racing and other forms of institutionalised gambling. Demand pushes up share prices and not surprisingly the market overheats from time to time. In February 1983 a dramatic slump in the market was triggered by the announcement of government plans to regulate unit trusts. Hundreds of small investors saw their inflated shares fall by 40, 50 and even 60 per cent. The three major banks do not suffer since they act as broker and banker, as well as investing on their own account, and they are in a better position than their customers to keep ahead of market trends. The stock market certainly mobilises capital, but it is generally agreed that better safeguards need to be devised to protect the small investor.

Warning signals have been flashing constantly in Israel ever since she came into existence. It is hardly surprising if she has become colour-blind. Perhaps she has been running so fast for so many years that her leaders do not know how to slow down. She is worried that the flow of immigrants has dwindled to a trickle. What will bring more immigrants and what will make them stay in the long run? What size does Israel want to be? What size should she want to be? There never was a people so self-analytical. Maybe there are no present answers to these questions. No nation can entirely shape its own history.

6

Foreign Policy

'Foreign policy is not made by lucid thinkers and contemplative planners, but by choices of priorities; reaction to events; aspirations and opportunities; decisions and avoidance of decisions; adherence to moral values and consideration of domestic issues.' The writer is Gideon Rafael, who spent twenty-five years in Israel's Foreign Ministry and as ambassador. Israel's foreign policy has, for the thirty-five years of her existence, been dominated by four factors: her geographical position, on a strategic frontier of the East-West power game where oil serves to raise the stakes and confuse the issues; the overt threat from neighbouring Arab states; her relative diplomatic isolation, not only in the Middle East but in the world community and more especially with Europe; and her dependence on foreign aid. This combination has fostered an '*ain brerah*' ('we have no choice') attitude to self-defence and, by extension, to other foreign policy decisions.

Israel's geographical position gave her the option of either trying to play the non-aligned pig in the middle between the superpowers of East and West, or placing herself squarely in the sphere of influence of either the Soviet Union or the United States. To the weak infant state only the first course lay open. To survive the initial years at all she had to become strong and seek arms from every possible source, and when she did become militarily strong she then constituted a threat to an Arab bloc which both East and West felt constrained to humour. In the event it was the Arabs, not Israel, who set about playing both sides off against the middle. Israel, partly for demographic reasons reaching back before her birth, and partly for more hard-headed strategic reasons, became irrevocably indebted to the United States. America's Middle East policy has lacked consistency ever since. This chapter will start by examining Israel's relations with the superpowers.

Europe's relations with Israel have been overshadowed by too much history. Post-war relations with Germany were a psychological minefield which both countries felt an urgent need to clear away. Britain's official attitude has been inconsistent, with traditional Foreign Office Arabophilia tempered by the pronouncements and pressures of a handful of pro-Zionist public figures. For her part Israel has retained a generous respect for Britain's (non-military) institutions while reserving profound distrust for her diplomatic inclinations in the Middle East. The Mandate left too many scars for there ever to exist between Britain and Israel that warmth which, for a time, characterised relations with France. In general the development of a European entity through the Common Market has proved an excluding factor for Israel. By and large Israel reproaches Europe for presuming that their long-view of events in the Middle East is in every respect juster and wiser than her own estimate formed by actually existing within the region. Israel's relations with Europe are considered in the second section of this chapter.

The perceived threat of annihilation at the hands of neighbouring Arab states, which two generations of policy-makers lived with, is sometimes dismissed by casual commentators as just another manifestation of national paranoia. Yet to deny that threat flies in the face of thirty years of vehement Arab declarations. 'The Arab national aim is the elimination of Israel' (Nasser, 1965 and 1967). 'The basic concern of the

Palestinian revolution is the uprooting of the Zionist society from our land and liberating it . . . supported by the iron fist of the Arab masses' (Arafat, 1980). Israel had no reason to believe this was empty rhetoric. She was also acutely aware of what a tiny state she is. 'The entire country is a frontier,' complained Dayan. War against Israel was, for nearly thirty years, a major integrating factor between her politically unstable Arab neighbours. The evolution of the Arab threat to Israel's security and its effects on Israel and Israelis will be the subject of the third section of this chapter.

Israel's anomalous position of aggressive military self-reliance concerning her own borders, and her recalcitrant economic dependence *vis-à-vis* the United States, coupled with the oil-based expedient Arabophilia of Western Europe and America, has driven Israel into international isolation. She sought a way out of this through contacts with the developing countries in the Third World, first in Asia and subsequently in Africa and Latin America. These overtures are the subject of section four of this chapter. If she can only settle the so-called Palestinian Question, that gesture could well open up the way to fresh contacts with the Third World.

Israel and the Superpowers

The years immediately after the Second World War opened up the possibility for the Soviet Union to enter the strategic area of the Middle East. It was not a region of which she had previous experience, and it took her a decade to decide firmly where her best interests lay. Her brief flirtation with Israel between 1947 and 1953 looks, in retrospect, like no more than a false opening gambit; but it was vital to Israel at a pre-eminently vulnerable point in her history.

The Soviet Union had been, after Czechoslovakia, the first country to enter into diplomatic relations with the new state, and even before that, in May 1947, while she was only halfheartedly supporting Arab independence movements, she saw her way to facilitating the sale of crucial quantities of captured and surplus German arms and ammunition through Czechoslovakia. A certain number of old Second World War fighter planes were also made available. The episode is treated with some reticence by the Russians, who subsequently thought better of it; by the Czechs, who, after the Slansky show trials, preferred to forget it; and by the British, who were at the time doing their best to prevent the arms reaching Palestine under the Mandate. It is interesting, above all, in the perspective of Soviet attitudes. By 1955 the relationship had chilled to the point where not Israel but Egypt became the beneficiary of a Czech arms deal with Soviet blessing.

How did the Soviet Union regard the Middle East in those early post-war years? Several of the small states there, Israel included, were in a post-colonial situation, and were, *ipso facto*, deserving of Soviet encouragement. On the face of it Israel, with her socialist traditions even before statehood and her European cultural heritage, was the more accessible. As regards the Arab states, the question was debated as to whether they were accessible to communism and could move directly from feudalism to communism without passing through the intermediate stage of capitalism. Mao had not yet tried this experiment in China. Soviet opinion tended to the affirmative, but experience had proved frustrating. The incentive to some sort of initiative in Israel was, on the one hand, the prospect of filling the power vacuum left by the withdrawal of British influence in the Eastern Mediterranean, and on the other hand a spirit of competition with the United States for the future allegiance of an emerging nation. If, in the process, she drove a wedge between the United States and Britain, so much the better.

One thing is certain: the Soviet Union was not and has never been deeply involved in the conflict between Israel and the Arab World. As Kammer points out, superpowers are, by definition, concerned with superpower politics. They have their priorities, as all non-superpowers learn to their cost sooner or later. Israel has persisted in playing the 'enfant terrible' in this context. While the Soviet Union was tentatively sending arms to a selection of Middle Eastern customers, Israel scoured world markets equally indiscriminately in her search for arms. Especially did she court the United States, for there she had the support of the largest Zionist group in the world. It contributed money in astonishing amounts, and lobbied and demonstrated to the extent that senators and successive presidents of the United States professed to be afraid of its voting power. So Israel played her American card for all it was worth and it proved to be a widow's cruse . . . In Soviet eyes, an Israel not entirely dependent on her for military aid would also be beyond her sphere of political domination. 'It can only be deduced', says Kammer, 'that the Kremlin, misled by the stock Marxist-Leninist view that Arab states were reactionary and colonially orientated, underestimated the potential strength of anti-Western sentiment in the Arab World. By the same token it over-estimated the advantages offered by support for the Jewish state. One thing is clear: the Soviet Union's basic impulse was opportunism.'

The disillusion was mutual. Israel felt that the Eastern block was being obstructive about the mass emigration she needed to build up the new state; emigration which the Soviet Union had facilitated in the initial years. 1952 saw the trial of Slansky, the Jewish Czech communist leader, and of 13 other top communist officials, 11 of them Jews, accused of disloyalty to the Stalinist régime through their 'collaboration with international Zionism'. The following year the so-called 'Doctors' Plot' brought the execution of Beria and a further wave of anti-Semitism in the Soviet Union, together with a corresponding reaction in Israel. Yet even in 1954–6 the Soviet Union was covering some 30–40 per cent of Israel's oil needs. Perhaps the Western-inspired

Baghdad Pact and the subsequent Bandung Conference of aspiring non-aligned nations in 1955, showed the Soviet leadership the anti-Western potential of the policy of non-alignment. By courting Nasser, Tito and Nehru it hoped to gain influence with the Third World. The following year Suez served to focus world opinion away from the Soviet suppression of the popular uprising in Hungary. By the mid 1950s the estrangement with Israel was more or less complete, even though it was not until the 1967 war that diplomatic relations were broken off.

Just how far would the Soviet Union incur the risk of a superpower conflict in the Middle East? Would she, as Terrence Prittie thinks, draw back, when the risk became apparent, from an area she does not fully understand? Or has she some proud design on the lines suggested by Gideon Rafael? His view is that the permanent Soviet challenge in the Middle East has only been kept in check by an implicit American show of force. 'On occasions when Soviet policy has over-reached itself,' he says, 'and created a direct threat to vital Western interests in the area, the United States has managed to rally and curb the Soviet challenge. Just as all the full-scale wars between the Arab states and Israel have been halted by cease-fire orders agreed upon by the two superpowers, even when they culminated, as in October 1973, in an American nuclear alert resolved by a mutual withdrawal from the brink, but not by an agreed political accommodation of their interests and aspirations in the area.' Rafael traces a steady Soviet encroachment to South Yemen and the Horn of Africa, with an eye to controlling the Straits of Hormuz, the gateway to the Persian Gulf. At the same time he sees the other half of the pincer being forged to the north through Iraq, already beholden to her for arms, and thence to Syria and Lebanon. The prospects for the Soviet strategy depend on a variety of factors: the internal stability of Iran, for instance; the general development of Soviet-Arab relations; future relations between Israel and Egypt; and

97

finally the Politburo's assessment of the American commitment to Israel's security and its determination to resist the execution of the Soviet grand design. It is not, perhaps, altogether surprising that a longstanding member of the Israeli Foreign Affairs establishment such as Rafael should adopt this line of argument, which could be seen as the most convincing case in favour of maximum and continued military aid to Israel by the United States.

Although the United States was one of the first countries to recognise the new state of Israel, this was largely a token of goodwill for the benefit of the Jewish lobby and an encouraging pat on the head for an emotive newcomer to the community of nations, a personal gesture by President Truman. But it was many years, some would say two decades, before the United States and the rest of the world took Israel seriously as a nation to be reckoned with.

There are three strands in America's attitude to Israel: the Zionist lobby, superpower strategy and oil. From Israel's point of view there is her long-term need for arms and economic aid, which has reached the point where the withholding of aid would, even in peacetime, put at risk the economic viability (and therefore the internal stability) of the state.

The actual influence of the Zionist lobby on United States policy has perhaps been over-rated. Even with those 3.5 million Jewish voters, the United States Government did nothing for Israel during the War of Independence or in the Sinai-Suez Campaign in 1956. Similarly, if there were no Jewish lobby the United States would still now be loath to abandon the one stable parliamentary democracy at the eastern end of the Mediterranean. But Israel has never been a passive protégé and has kept American reactions on a sliding scale between diplomatic embarrassment and exasperation. 'How', asked George Ball recently, 'did we get into the present situation of dependence without responsibility?'

The relationship has certainly evolved since the early days

of Secretary of State Dulles, who firmly refused arms to Israel altogether; or the days when, in 1957, President Eisenhower actually forced Israel to pull her troops out of Sinai. It was only after the Suez exploit that Dulles, and presumably a section of the State Department, decided that a strong Israel could, by holding down the bulk of Egypt's armed forces, serve the purpose of restricting Nasser's freedom of action. In the early 1960s Kennedy inaugurated a new phase in Israeli-American relations by publicly approving Israel's purchase of Hawk surface-to-air missiles, although at that time the understanding was that Israel could only be supplied with defensive weapons. President Johnson subsequently agreed to provide offensive weapons: tanks and fighter-bombers. These were the years of Eshkol's New Economic Policy, wherein the defence ministry played an important role. Peres visited President Johnson, with and without Eshkol. He made useful and lasting contacts in America. Sisco continued for many years after to be a friendly ally in the State Department. Israel acquired the planes, the tanks and the weapons she asked for, and also the expertise and machinery for making them herself. It was already obvious in the 1960s, to those with eyes to see, that sooner or later America was going to find herself with conflicting interests in the Middle East, and for her own peace of mind Israel's aim had to be material self-sufficiency in her defence requirements.

After Israel's spectacular victory in the Six-Day War of 1967, the United States began to see her not simply as territory but as a power. Americans will admit they like a winner and a victorious David against Goliath was doubly attractive. But Israel has often lacked the diplomatic skill to make the most of her military successes. Her diplomacy has tended too often to be confined simply to stating her own maximal demands rather than entering into a realistic dialogue with either friends or adversaries. It could be argued that in this she is merely imitating her neighbours. All one

99

can say is that it is not a sign of confidence or maturity. In 1967 the Minister of Defence admitted that the reason for the government's reluctance to state its position on peace proposals was that it simply had no policy on the matter. Israel's political leaders have too often appeared absorbed in domestic strife when the international situation cried out for broader vision.

Israel can never forget that she is a very small country, barely able to make ends meet even with foreign aid, and a potential battleground for a superpower confrontation. Nasser's death in 1970 cooled the situation temporarily, but the accession of Sadat to the Egyptian presidency was not at first reassuring; Sadat too needed a dramatic victory to consolidate his position. Rabin was in Washington at this time and said he could see where the War of Attrition was leading American policy and was horrified. He meant that he foresaw ever-increasing pressure on Israel to appease her neighbours. It was not a temporary phenomenon. The Yom Kippur War of 1973 shook Israel's self-confidence as well as her military foundations. Ultimate victory was wrested narrowly out of the jaws of disaster. Scapegoats were sought and found: military intelligence, Defence Minister Dayan, Prime Minister Golda Meir. The post mortem of the Agranat Commission was destructive and sapped still further Israel's faith in her decision-makers. Admittedly her military unpreparedness was inexcusable, but those who deplored, in retrospect, her lack of initiative, were perhaps failing to appreciate her predicament. She seemed to have spent so much energy resisting American pressure to pursue policies she was convinced were against her best interests, that she lacked the drive to formulate initiatives of her own.

The predominantly Arab oil states set up OPEC in 1973, and American anxiety to foster good relations with them was colouring deeper every year her view of the Middle East strategic situation. Just what effects the oil factor had on events in the Middle East is not easy to assess. It has been suggested that it may have encouraged Egypt and Syria to take the offensive against Israel in the belief that the Gulf and North African oil states were ready to use oil as a political weapon in support of their own military action. For example, Egypt and Syria may well have received encouragement from Saudi Arabia for the military action they took in 1973. Political leadership within the Arab World could pass from the Cairo-Damascus military axis to a new oil-based alliance of Riyadh, Tripoli and Baghdad. Arguably, at the end of the October War in 1973, it was to avoid oil damage to its own and its allies' energy economies that the United States hastened to bring such unprecedented pressure to bear on Israel to accept a cease-fire. 'The events of 1973', says Smart, 'have revealed the possession by Arab states of an instrument potentially capable over time of forcing one superpower, in effective collaboration with another, to impose on Israel a settlement acceptable to its adversaries.' And this, despite the fact that the United States was one of the nations least vulnerable to an Arab embargo, in that only 7 per cent of her oil came from Arab sources.

A more interesting aspect of the oil factor is the proportion of additional revenue generated by high OPEC prices since 1974 which is spent on arms. The Soviet Union has less high technology and attractive weapons to offer rich Arab states than America has, and she is less able to furnish them with the sophisticated industrial equipment they want. United States influence in the Middle East, therefore, may well increase – but at the expense of uncharted shifts in the military balance of power.

Henry Kissinger was the United States' special envoy who conducted three long bouts of shuttle diplomacy between 1973 and 1977 with a view to reconciling irreconcilables. He did not succeed. His main function was to put pressure on Israel to withdraw from territory occupied during the war, in Sinai, on the Golan Heights and in Jerusalem. Israel, basking in the sense of security imparted by her extended

101

frontiers, was loath to concede any of it. The most logical reason given for this was that she hesitated to surrender in advance any cards she might find useful in future direct negotiations. She was, in any case, adamant about staying in Jerusalem and on the Golan. Eventually she wrung from Kissinger a promise to try to place the supply of arms to Israel on a long-term basis, and also the crucial commitment that America would support Israel in reaction against possible guerilla attacks originating from Syrian territory. Since Palestinian guerillas were making regular sorties across the northern border, this was not abstract diplomacy. Nevertheless, Israel gave not an inch on the territorial issue. And in a sense she was right, in that the moment was not, from Israel's point of view, ripe. It was to ripen after Sadat's Jerusalem visit. The fact that Israel still did not use her obstinately reserved cards even then is another matter.

When Kissinger left for the last time in 1977 he was reproachful: 'We've tried to reconcile our support for you with our other interests in the Middle East,' he told Peres. He was also pessimistic about America's whole superpower strategy in the area: 'The United States will be discredited . . . We're losing control. We'll now see the Arabs working on a united front. There will be more emphasis on the Palestinians, and there will be a linkage between moves in the Sinai and on the Golan. The Soviets will accelerate their relations with the Arabs.' And he was mildly threatening: 'There will be pressures to drive a wedge between Israel and the United States, not because we want that, but because it will be in the dynamic of the situation.' He was only partly right. The forthright approach announced by the newly elected President Carter in 1977 might have born some fruits with the old Labour leadership in Israel, worn down by Kissinger, but it failed to get the measure of Israel's new right-wing Likud government and of its leader Menachem Begin. Begin vowed from the start not to retreat from the Gaza Strip or from Judea and Samaria (as he termed the

West Bank territories) and to consider compromise in Sinai and the Golan only in the context of an overall peace. It went without saying that he would never consider leaving Jerusalem. He has not moved from that position.

'When Begin met Sadat in Jerusalem,' wrote Gideon Rafael, both knew where they wanted to go, but not how to get there.' Would it not have been possible for Israel to achieve the given result without waiting for the intervention of the United States? To have concluded a Treaty of Jerusalem instead of a Camp David Accord? Sadat, for his part, had probably banked on American assistance. Perhaps it was even convenient for him to be able to give the impression of having his arm twisted a little. But surely there was some way Begin could have emerged with more international credit? He seems to have seen only the electoral image he was creating for himself among one half of the population at home, but never apparently stepped out of that narrow context to consider the image of Israel he was creating in the world at large. He is not alone in this. Israeli politicians are a highly active parochial group in a small country. Their most popular Foreign Minister and diplomat outside Israel has been Abba Eban, a polished, witty intellectual who explained his country's idiosyncrasies with brilliant success abroad, and tried vainly to do the same thing at home. He was not appreciated. So Begin, apparently grudgingly, put his hand eventually to the Camp David Agreement, on American soil, and President Carter took the limelight. America gained an implicit right to intervene in any future situation in which Camp David could be invoked.

The settlement of the question of a state or homeland for the Palestinians, refugees and otherwise, was a case in point. It was relegated to the margin of the Camp David negotiations, but Egypt has never ceased to call on the United States to press Israel to move on the subject. The Arab bloc has realised this is Israel's weakest point and the best focus for isolating her from her potential friends. George Ball has

103

no doubt about this: 'The blunt fact is that as long as Israel holds on to the Occupied Territories, and especially so long as it seems to be seeking to consolidate its hold on the West Bank for the long term, its impact on the stability of the Middle East will be wholly negative.' Israel is still doing just that; leaving the State Department baffled by the fact of Israel's dependence on the United States for arms and economic aid, and yet her wilful disregard of American advice.

America's worst fears must have been realised in the summer of 1982 when, at the high point of the Peace for Galilee Operation, the Israeli Army had swept forward in three days to the outskirts of Beirut. Every day came news of her finding vast stockpiles of Soviet arms. She looked set to completely destroy the PLO as a military force. She had her man, Bashir Gemayel, ready to set in place. She had to be cut down to size. Throughout the West the media was solidly anti-Israel even before the bombing of Beirut, long before the incidents at Chatilla and Sabra camps. It was even hinted at the height of the campaign that the American Government might have entertained the possibility of actually conniving at the fall of Begin's government in order to see it replaced by a more flexible Labour Alignment government; and so precarious was the state of Israel's economy that this would have been technically possible. But it did not happen; and one logical reason why it did not is that, whatever the international reaction to his policies, Begin still had the popular support of a sizeable majority of the population at home. In an increasingly volatile area Israel is still undeniably an oasis of stable, comprehensible Western-style democracy.

Israel and Europe

The first generations of Jewish immigrants from Europe not unnaturally continued to consider themselves European in

104

their cultural values. They adopted a European model of parliamentary government, set up European-style economic institutions, and even if their brand of socialism did not actually exist in Europe, their aspirations had been nurtured in a European environment. Israel's early leaders repudiated any charges of 'Levantinisation', and in so far as they had time to see Israel in her geographical context they envisaged her as an oasis of civilisation in a backward region, demonstrating how to make the desert bloom, given enough toil, inventiveness and determination. Understandably engrossed in her own security and economic development, Israel even now stands poised between self-absorption and an almost morbid concern about her image in the rest of the world.

Britain has rarely known how to retain the respect and friendship of countries she has administered as colonies or under some other form of tutelage, except where they have been peopled with British emigrants. For Israel, the manner in which the Mandate was ended left a taste of ashes. In May 1950, at the Lausanne Conference, Britain, France and the United States made a half-hearted attempt to restore some stability to the Middle East, and it was after this meeting that the much-quoted Tripartite Declaration was issued. 'Should the three governments find that any one of these states (Israel or her Arab neighbours) contemplates violating the frontiers of the Armistice lines, they will . . . act both within and without the framework of the United Nations in order to prevent such a violation.' In 1950 it was not Israel who was likely to do the violating. Weapons, continued the Declaration, would be rationed to all Middle Eastern nations, and then only for legitimate self-defence and 'to permit them to play their part in the defence of the area as a whole'. Israel found this reassuring, even while she recognised in it an element of Tripartite self-interest.

This marked a high-point in Anglo-Israeli relations. The following year General Sir Brian Robertson, Commander-in-Chief of British Forces in the Middle East, paid an official visit to Tel Aviv with the aim of obtaining access to harbours and bases for the British Navy and RAF. Ben Gurion even briefly visualised the possibility of a Commonwealth-type relationship on the New Zealand model, but this was short-lived. When Eden's Conservative government came to office in 1951 British favours swung to Egypt. By 1953 London was seconding Washington's efforts to put pressure on Israel to make territorial concessions to Egypt in order to win Egyptian participation in a Middle East Defence Pact. The reassurances of the Tripartite Declaration were already beginning to wear thin. By 1956 they had been erased alto-gether. Washington announced that in the event of an Arab-Israeli war it would place major emphasis on acting through the United Nations; which meant subjecting enforcement measures to a Soviet veto in the Security Council. This was one month before the Suez operation. At this same juncture Britain could not make up her mind how to deal with the Arab League and the charismatic Egyptian leader, Gamal Nasser. While Israel distrusted Britain as a diplomatic ally, as a source of arms she found her almost a non-starter. She received a few outdated Meteor jets in the early 1950s, but Britain's important arms markets were and are the Arab states. The Suez episode left Britain with her political leader-ship embarrassed and confused, and her economic and strat-egic interests in the Middle East severely damaged. Since then Britain's relations with Israel have been conducted largely within the framework of the European-Israeli relationship.

With France, on the other hand, Israel enjoyed a decade of genuinely warm relations from the mid 1950s to the mid '60s. This was largely due to Shimon Peres and a coincidental concentration of Jews in strategic government and adminis-trative positions in France, which may or may not have influenced policies but which certainly facilitated common understanding. France had had her own Arab problems to contend with ever since the end of the Second World War, when longstanding Muslim nationalist movements flared up in French North Africa. The culmination of this had been the accession to power of Sultan Sidi Mohammed in an independent Morocco in 1955, and of President Bourguiba in an independent Tunisia in 1956. In Algeria, where nearly 1.25 million Frenchmen had settled, a nationalist revolt in 1954 degenerated into a stalemate of ugly guerilla warfare, costly in lives, money and morale. France and Israel could be said to have had a common interest in deflating the figurehead of Arab nationalism, President Nasser.

Operation Musketeer was the name given to a secret Anglo-French venture whose object was to guarantee by military force the renewal of international sovereignty over the Suez Canel, which Nasser had nationalised. Israel was more interested in the Straits of Tiran, and the approaches to her own port of Eilat, than in Suez itself, but she naturally took an interest in the possibility of joint action – if not in the objectives of the war, then at least in its timing. Ben Gurion, according to Peres, trusted the sincerity of France, but he was suspicious of Britain's intentions. He saw in Eden the founder and patron of the Arab League and believed that the Anglo-Jordanian pact would one day work against Israel. So secret talks were held at a private villa at Sèvres on the outskirts of Paris, with the French trying to manoeuvre Israel into playing the key role, while the English did their best to keep their hands clean and talked of Churchill's time-honoured principle that partnership between allied armies should be bound up with the independent political objectives of warring nations. Ben Gurion became convinced that his anxieties were well founded. They wanted Israel to provide the pretext; and then the British could intervene to separate the so-called aggressors, Egypt and Israel. Israel insisted that this was out of the question. However, agreement was reached and signed at Sèvres.

The key to Operation Musketeer, from Israel's point of view, was that while her army mobilised, the French and British Airforces knocked out the Egyptian Airforce on the ground, thus protecting Israel's major cities. Israel then launched her limited offensive on the Canal, 'more than a raid, less than a war' as Dayan put it, and went on to carry out her own objectives; namely the capture of Sharm el Sheikh to reopen the Straits of Tiran and the destruction of the Egyptian Army.

The Sinai Campaign was an unmitigated success in military terms. Diplomatically it raised a dust-storm; for Dulles, ostensibly concerned about international law and the United Nations Charter, but in fact anxious about American-Arab relations; for Moscow, deeply involved in the Hungarian uprising and angered at the humiliation of her protégé and the loss of so much Soviet armoury. Eden bowed to pressures at home and from across the Atlantic and called for a cease-fire. The French could not sustain Operation Musketeer alone. Within three months the Canal Zone had been placed under a United Nations Peace-keeping Force, and for both France and Britain the Suez episode was over. Under severe international pressure Israel reluctantly evacuated Sinai early the following year, and conducted a rearguard action within the United Nations under the able baton of Abba Eban. The whole episode had merely confirmed Israel's distrust of Britain, her relative empathy with France, and her realisation that she was but a single pawn in the world strategy of the United States.

Israel built on her relationship with France for some years after Suez. French military equipment flowed into Israel, and France was the chief supplier of Israel's fast-growing airforce. From France's point of view Israel was a useful proving-ground for her Mirage jets and later for her Matra air-to-air missiles, just as today she is a proving-ground for American military hardware. In the late 1950s there was also joint Franco-Israeli research in the nuclear field, and in

1957 an agreement enabled French private industry to assist Israel in constructing her first nuclear reactor at Dimona. 'At a cost of $75 million the reactor was clearly intended for more than civilian research,' comments Sachar. With the advent in 1958 of De Gaulle to the presidency there came a cooling of Franco-Israeli friendship, and by the mid 1960s it was no longer the nostalgia of the Operation Musketeer alliance which dominated France's attitude to Israel, but rather the twin forums of NATO and the European Economic Community.

It was, in fact, Germany, not France, who supported Israel's unsuccessful attempts to gain admission to the EEC. Ironically, Israel's first sustained contacts with Europe had been with the German Federal Republic. They developed out of the Luxembourg Reparations Agreement, signed in 1952 by Chancellor Adenauer and Israeli Foreign Minister Moshe Sharett. The agreed figure was $862 million in money and goods over twelve years. This, of course, excluded claims for individual restitution by Holocaust victims. The settlement was opposed by many Christian Democrats in Germany on the grounds that it would help to build up the Israeli economy and facilitate the survival of the new state in the face of hostile Arab neighbours with whom Germany did a good deal of trade and where she wished to invest. Whether delivered with good or bad grace, reparations were, as we saw in the chapter on the economy, a much-needed shot in the arm for the Israeli economy.

Israel regarded German weapons as hardly less important than German funds. As early as 1957 Peres opened negotiations with the German Defence Minister, Franz Josef Strauss. By early 1959 German weapons began to flow to Israel, via France and under cover of secrecy so as not to offend Arab sensibilities. Relations were cordial, though not exactly warm. The trial in 1960 of Adolf Eichmann, one of the most prominent architects of the German Final Solution to the Jewish Problem, had the unexpected effect of promoting a new understanding between the two countries. The unspeakable past relations between Germans and Jews was, for many months, matter for public debate. In the person of Eichmann Israel subjected the German nation to trial and judgement. It was a cathartic, though not exactly a healing experience. After it the way was open to more normal relations between the two countries.

The early 1960s were the period when Israel was making a determined effort to fight her way out of international isolation through practical multilateral co-operation. Germany was one of her first targets. She opened negotiations for a substantial low-interest loan. Adenauer was at that time seeking a friendly reception in the United States. 'A photographed handshake with Ben Gurion', says Sachar, 'could make all the difference in the Chancellor's reception; . . . for that single gesture of Jewish reconciliation the sum of $250 million was ridiculously low.' The eventual figure came to over $350 million in annual instalments, each earmarked for a major development project of Israel's choice, chiefly new towns in the Negev. As a result of reparations and loans, trade with Germany expanded rapidly in the early 1960s, though with a growing imbalance partly due to EEC restrictions on Israeli exports to Germany. Strauss's secret arms deal was renewed regularly by his successors, and in addition to German arms large quantities of American arms, including tanks and anti-aircraft missiles, were reaching Israel via Germany. When, in 1964, the press got wind of the secret arms deals, there were angry reactions from Germany's Arab trading partners and it became evident that shipments would have to cease. The price Israel demanded for this was diplomatic recognition, coupled with an agreement that America would continue to fulfil Germany's arms commitments while Germany would continue to foot the bill. In May 1965 diplomatic relations were formally opened between Israel and Germany and three months later the first ambassadors were exchanged. A bitter chapter in Jewish and German history was formally closed.

In the early 1960s Israel found her bilateral relations with France and Germany losing ground before NATO and the EEC. The Common Market of Western Europe was Israel's best hope for expanding her trade. North America involved heavy transport costs. Trade with Britain had declined from about 30 per cent of Israel's total in 1950 to about 12 per cent in 1968. Trade with Eastern Europe seemed unlikely to increase. Yet trade with the EEC countries faced a unified tariff barrier. Associate membership, already granted to Spain, Greece, Turkey and the North African countries, would have offered preferential status *vis-à-vis* the Common Market. In 1960, after persistent efforts, Israel had been granted a 20 per cent tariff reduction on quotas of certain industrial products, though not on her major hard-currency earners like eggs, citrus fruit, tyres and plywood. The Defence Ministry, through its procurement network, found one means of circumventing EEC barriers by employing the operational methods of some American companies in Europe; special trade arrangements involving production under licence and joint stock sharing were entered into by individual Israeli and European corporations, at first in weapons and aircraft production and electronics, but later in a wider sphere of activities.

In 1973 the OPEC price war overshadowed the Dublin Conference of EEC Foreign Ministers. They also had Middle East security in mind, and initiated a 'global Mediterranean policy' to replace their existing bilateral agreements with countries like Spain, Algeria, Tunisia, Morocco and Israel. Such a policy would be translated into concessionary tariffs for those countries in their trade with the EEC. This eventually led to the Brussels Trade Pact of May 1975. Israel gained an initial 60 per cent concession and a promise of further reductions to come. She saw it as a major

111

breakthrough. But by the same stroke the Trade Pact opened up the Israeli market to foreign competition. It meant a major challenge to Israeli industrial efficiency. And at the same time the EEC started to express a collective opinion about the 'legitimate rights of the Palestinians' and to call upon Israel to withdraw to her pre-1967 frontiers. At every EEC summit conference came exhortations for a 'just and lasting peace' in the Middle East, for 'respect for the sovereignty and independence of every state in the area', for 'the right to live in peace within secure and recognised frontiers'. The phrases were relatively meaningless because Europe had, jointly and severally, helped to create an irreconcilable territorial situation in the Middle East. No amount of exhortation could produce justice for all parties. Europe, and not only Germany, had a guilty conscience about the Jews, just as Israel had a guilty conscience about the Palestinians. But it was just as futile for Europe to wish Israel would disappear as it was for the Israelis to wish the Palestinians would disappear. The empty phrases only strengthened Israeli paranoia. Europe's apparent faith in a United Nations framework and its provenly ineffective peace-keeping forces was not helpful.

In June 1980 the seventeenth annual meeting of the EEC Heads of State (the European Council) took place in Venice. A fresh initiative was launched to open a 'Euro-Arab dialogue at all levels' and to this end the Council issued what has since been referred to as the Venice Declaration. The focus was to be on a 'comprehensive settlement under the four headings of withdrawal (by Israel to pre-1967 frontiers), self-determination (for Palestinian Arabs), security in the Middle East (in global terms), and Jerusalem; 'these to form a coherent whole'. It is not clear why they had to form a coherent whole, unless it was that a veto on one item could be interpreted as rejection of any possible agreement under the other headings. The clear implication was that all these aims were to be brought about by Israeli concessions. The

112

EEC seems to have aspired, in the words of the Declaration, 'to providing a more consistent platform designed to bring the parties concerned closer together.' This would seem, on the face of it, to be misguided. Israeli-Arab relations are a regional problem of good-neighbourliness, or they are a superpower problem on the frontier between East and West; Europe has very little surviving authority there.

Israel and her Arab neighbours

Israel is so small compared with her neighbours and the level of their hostility has been so great that relations with them have been virtually confined to military operations, their preparation and aftermath. Diplomatic relations are not possible between a country and neighbours who do not recognise her right to exist. For thirty years survival occupied the foreground. Israel, they will tell you there, was created to solve the Jewish problem, not the Arab problem. Nevertheless, it has been her avowed policy to make peace with her neighbours, if possible, tackling them one by one. A good deal on this subject has crept into other sections of the book, so here the object is only to give a brief outline of Israel's foreign policy towards her neighbours: Egypt, Jordan, Syria and Lebanon.

Egypt was an interested party as far back as the Rhodes Armistice Agreement in 1949 when Israel's 'pre-1967 borders' were drawn. They followed the old border of the Ottoman Palestine with an enclave round the Palestinian Arab town of Gaza, now known as the Gaza Strip. Thereafter, Israel showed no special interest in Egypt until the Czech arms deal of 1955. The Suez-Sinai Campaign in the following year demonstrated how easily the Egyptian Army could be defeated. Nevertheless, as President Nasser consolidated his position in Egypt, he assumed the leadership

113

of the Arab World and as its spokesman encouraged its own belligerency. In 1964 he espoused the Palestinian cause, began to fund the PLO and encouraged border raids on Israel. Israel now regarded Egypt as her most threatening neighbour. In 1967 Nasser, confident that he had an army capable of destroying Israel and, in his own words, 'cleansing the Arab World', launched his concerted attack. It led to a catastrophic defeat for him and considerable loss of prestige.

For the next six years Israel's military and political leaders, in a spirit of euphoria, slackened their defences. When, in 1970, Nasser died and was succeeded by President Anwar Sadat, Israel was unimpressed. Then, in 1973, she was caught by surprise by the Yom Kippur attack and jolted out of her complacency. Even though she rallied and fought back to eventual victory, she was forced to negotiate with Egypt over the post-war territorial settlement. In 1977, shortly after Begin became Prime Minister, Sadat, too, felt confident enough to respond to Israel's approaches and fly to Jerusalem. Israel and Egypt had entered a period of diplomatic relations as distinct from tactical and strategic military relations. It was a moment for Israel to be magnanimous and statesman-like and she failed to rise to the occasion. It seemed that she had grown so accustomed to confrontation that her right-wing leaders were incapable of a more flexible response. Begin's intransigence drained the impetus of Sadat's courageous initiative until it was almost exhausted, and needed the intervention of President Carter to push it through to a conclusion. As a result of the protracted Camp David negotiations, Egypt recovered Sinai, while Israel needlessly lost a good deal of international sympathy and naïvely assumed that by relinquishing Sinai she was paving the way to international approval of her annexation of certain other occupied territories in the future. All in all, she did not make the Egyptian precedent a particularly encouraging one which neighbouring states might be prepared to follow.

114

Jordan had the benefit of Glubb's Arab Legion when it invaded Israel in 1949 and ended up controlling the West Bank, which she subsequently annexed. The fact that Jordan occupied territory so near the Israeli heartland, meant that Israel's relations with her acquired a different dimension from those with her other Arab neighbours. Israel had to be sure that Jordan never became a serious military threat; but at the same time Jordan being herself a weak power in the area, was anxious not to provoke Israel – until 1967. Before the Six-Day War Israel had assured King Hussein that if he refrained from attacking Israel, then she would not attack him and he would keep the West Bank. Hussein miscalculated Israel's chances of victory and did attack. The result, for him, was disastrous. Israel occupied Jerusalem and the West Bank territory and kept it after the war ended. The resulting exodus of PLO fighters from the West Bank into Jordan became a serious destabilising factor in Jordan where the PLO set about consolidating their position as a state within a state. By 1970 internal tension in Jordan had reached such a pitch that Hussein, with the support of his loyal bedouin army, expelled the PLO, who moved into Syria and Lebanon.

Meanwhile, in Israel, there had been debate about the nature of the new eastern frontier on the line of the river Jordan. Dayan, always an advocate of multiple Arab-Jewish relations at grass-roots level, won the day for his 'open bridges' policy, both on human and practical grounds, since so many people had family ties on both sides of the river. The bridges across the Jordan have remained open ever since, in peacetime. Thus plans to link Jordan with the West Bank are not drawn on a *tabula rasa*. Commercial and trade bonds are strong. There is little doubt that if Israel were to favour any solution regarding the future of the West Bank other than annexation, she would naturally favour some form of linkage with Jordan. This, it is assumed, would offer some prospect of creating an autonomous area of settlement for

115

the many Palestinians who would be prepared to accept such a 'homeland'. An additional advantage, in Israeli eyes, is that such an agreement could eventually be negotiated with King Hussein over the heads of the PLO leadership.

Syria has adopted a consistently hard line against Israel. Their common frontier was agreed at the Rhodes Armistice Talks in 1949 at the end of the War of Independence, but since it left Syrian troops at the foot of the Golan Heights overlooking the Galilee towns and settlements, it was obviously only temporary until the next inevitable war. There followed years of intermittent sniping and harassment on both sides of the line. In 1956 the Syrians had no time to mobilise their forces to play a part in the Suez-Sinai Campaign. In 1967 Israeli troops swept up to the top of the Golan Heights and established a new frontier there with Israelis now overlooking the Syrian capital of Damascus. Three years later, when the PLO was expelled from Jordan, many of them took up positions in Syria whence they launched sporadic operations against Israel. Israel's answer to this was massive retaliatory attacks on PLO bases, which curbed their activities but could not eradicate the source. In the 1973 war the Syrians advanced right across the Golan plateau before Israel could rally and push their front line to within fifteen miles of Damascus. One of the decisions taken at the ensuing Geneva Peace Conference was to set up a United Nations Peace-keeping Force along a border area on the Syrian side of the Golan.

For the next ten years there were no open hostilities between Israel and Syria. On the other hand, there has not been any constructive diplomatic activity either. President Assad has spurned all Israeli invitations to follow Sadat's example and make a journey to Jerusalem. This is partly because he has been preoccupied with chronic domestic divisions, which have been exploited by the extremist Muslim Brotherhood, and only with difficulty and an occa-

116

sional resort to armed force has Assad kept order within his own frontiers. The influx of PLO fighters from Lebanon in the autumn of 1982 after the Israeli seige of Beirut will not have eased these internal tensions, and it is hardly surprising that Assad did not feel in a position to offer asylum to Arafat and the PLO leadership at that time. On the whole, despite her hostility to Israel, Syria has done little more than passively react to events outside her borders. This in turn may well be because she is inhibited by her links with the Soviet Union. In the heyday of her alliance with Nasser's Egypt, and excluded as she was from Western arms markets, she turned to the Soviet Union for arms. She would not seem to have derived any great benefit from this relationship and she now finds herself a pawn in superpower politics. In fact, today, Syria should not be regarded as a key factor in the area, except in terms of superpower rivalry.

From 1948 to 1970 Lebanon posed no military threat to Israel. The 'good fence' border between the two countries was open to limited traffic and there were relatively few incidents. After Black September in 1970, when Palestinians from Jordan settled in camps in southern Lebanon, border incidents multiplied. A terrorist campaign was launched even outside the region; planes were hijacked, the Israeli Olympic team was assassinated at the Munich Games, and the Israeli-Lebanese border was turned into a confrontation area where attack was followed by retaliation and counter-retaliation. The PLO were not the only destabilising force in Lebanon; there were also the demographic changes described in chapter 2. From a combination of forces, therefore, by 1975 the central administration in Lebanon had disintegrated into religious factions and armed groups and the country had collapsed into civil war.

In 1978 Israel decided to make a bid to establish a more defensible northern frontier, a cordon sanitaire between herself and the Palestinians in Lebanon. She aimed at *de*

117

facto annexation of an area as far north as the Litani River. But the operation was inadequately planned, both militarily and diplomatically, and was condemned by America. Before the end of the year Israeli forces withdrew to the old international frontier and a United Nations Peacekeeping Force was installed in the zone between that frontier and the Litani River. Lacking confidence in the effectiveness of the United Nations Force to protect her own border settlements from raids, Israel supported and equipped Major Hadad, leader of a Christian Arab faction, to patrol the immediate border zone. But it must be emphasised that all this activity was conducted by the Army and under the ultimate sanction of the Defence Ministry; there was apparently very little contact between the Foreign Affairs Departments of the two countries. The same could be said of Operation Peace for Galilee, launched in June 1982. For months prior to this, Israeli border settlements had been under almost constant rocket attack by the Palestinians, despite the presence of the United Nations Force, while Israel had been launching intermittent reprisal air-raids on Lebanese coastal towns and suspected PLO strongholds. The immediate aim of the operation was to take the pressure off the Galilee settlements, and for this it had the whole-hearted support of the people. It was also an acknowledged fact that the PLO constituted a focus of emotional cohesion for the Arab World against Israel, and there were some Israeli military leaders who reasoned that if the PLO were ever to be destroyed as a potential military force, then the way might be opened for Israel to continue her policy of long-term bilateral rapprochement with her neighbours. From this point of view Operation Peace for Galilee was a success. But the aftermath was not diplomacy. It was simply a succession of military negotiations about troop withdrawals, observation forces and cooling-off periods. No real hopes were entertained about finding a long-term political solution.

118

Israel and the Third World

Israel, according to Abba Eban, has never been able to decide whether she is a European country in spirit, tradition, political institutions and economic ties, or an Asian country by reason of her geographical position. At the same time Eban was arguing vehemently in favour of Israel's admission to the EEC. It is all a question of self-image. Israel started with all the qualifications for membership of the Third World: a history of anti-colonialist revolt; few raw materials; a predominantly agricultural economy; a poor, uneducated immigrant minority in her population; and an acute shortage of capital. On the other hand a country so earnestly on its guard against Levantinisation was hardly disposed to see itself as a true member of the Third World. She set herself up as a challenging example to other poor nations of what could be achieved given the social and political will to survive and succeed. Israel's leaders did not seem to appreciate how this failed to endear them to other equally poor emergent nations. Nor did they see that their diplomatic support for the United States in the Korean War was bound to cast a shadow over any friendly advances they might make in the Far East at that time.

Israel's early contacts with the Third World were at best a qualified success. On Nehru of India she pinned high hopes at one time, but he had to contend with a Muslim minority at home and an aggressively Muslim neighbour, Pakistan; he delayed even recognition of Israel until 1950. With Japan diplomatic relations were opened in 1952, and with Burma in 1953. A very active period of relations with Burma grew almost by chance from a visiting trade delegation. David HaCohen, a prominent Mapai leader, was sent out as ambassador, and a multiplicity of channels were opened for trade, technical assistance and training. The limitless trade potential of China lay only a diplomatic step beyond Burma and at one time China seemed willing, but

119

fear of American disfavour apparently intimidated Israel. The opportunity passed unexplored. In 1955, when Tito, Nasser and Nehru attended the Bandung Conference of emerging Third World countries, Israel was not even invited. Zionism, rightly or wrongly, was identified in their minds with the West, and even, ironically, with Western imperialism; an impression which was only reinforced the following year by the Suez-Sinai Campaign.

Israel then transferred her attention to Africa and, less intensively, to South America. In the late 1950s non-alignment was replacing anti-colonialism as the rallying cry of the Third World. Again Israel had all the qualifications for membership of this evolving club, at least in the early years. In an attempt to seek a way out of diplomatic isolation, Israel expended a great deal of energy on technical co-operation with the other self-styled non-aligned nations. The post-Suez opening of the Gulf of Aqaba gave Israel a sea-route to Asia and Africa. She had much to offer: recent experience in desert agriculture, irrigation schemes and community development with backward immigrant peoples. Israelis had a common egalitarian touch in human relations, they rarely patronised, and they evinced a puritanical appetite for hard work. Also, the relatively modest scale of Israeli development schemes was, on the face of it, well suited to Third World nations wishing to set up their own self-help programmes. The Histadrut opened an Afro-Asian Institute for Labour Studies and Co-operation and thousands of Third World visitors attended its four- and eight-week training programmes. Israeli technical advisers were sometimes invited back to supervise schemes on site. Ghana was an enthusiastic client at one time; also Tanzania, Mali, Ethiopia, Zaire and Nigeria. Trade between Israel and African states expanded in the early 1960s. Diamonds from Zaire helped Tel Aviv become the world's major diamond centre; uranium, too, was supplied by Zaire. As her home industrial base developed, Israel began to offer military aid to her customers. Having established her own merchant shipping line (Zim) in the early 1950s, she was well placed to assist Ghana in doing the same. And how fortunate it was for her that she had helped to construct the airfield at Entebbe, when she launched her spectacular rescue operation on the hijacked plane there. Perhaps the Israelis were just too ambitious. They saw themselves as living refutation of the argument that poor countries stay poor because they are poor. But her very success was her undoing. When she began to look like one of the developed nations, she lost her attraction for the Third World. David seemed to have become Goliath.

In 1963 the Organisation for African Unity (OAU) came into being, and although in the early years many of its members kept ties with both Israel and the Arab World, the situation deteriorated. Many African states contain a strong Muslim element. In the United Nations General Assembly, too, the Third World, under Arab leadership, was finding and using its voice. Israel was identified with South Africa while the PLO was seen as a down-trodden minority fighting a neo-colonial power. In 1971 the six Arab members of the OAU (Algeria, Egypt, Libya, Morocco, Tunis and the Sudan) were contributing over a third of the organisation's revenue and putting Muslims in many key positions. In 1973 the Algiers Arab Summit placed an oil embargo on Israel (together with other states) but set up a development bank to assist African states with an initial grant of $200 million. Israel could not compete, and that same year the Yom Kippur War sealed her failure in Africa. From then onwards the Arab states espoused the cause of the Palestinians, about whose fate they had successfully hardened their hearts for the previous twenty-five years. They now focused attention on the contrast between Israel's emphasis on peace and democratic ideals, and her behaviour in the Occupied Territories of Gaza and the West Bank. In 1975 Israel was very nearly expelled from the United Nations.

121

There have recently been signs that, with the eclipse of Egypt in the Arab World and the dispersion of the PLO, parts of the Third World are responding to renewed Israeli approaches, notably in Africa and Central America. In view of the political climate in both areas the emphasis has been as much on arms and military equipment as on peaceful economic co-operation. In May 1982 Zaire was the first Black African country to renew diplomatic relations with Israel. The following year it was announced that Israel would assist in remodelling Mobutu's army, which would, naturally, be equipped with several million dollars' worth of Israeli arms.

In the past there was little Israel could do to attenuate her diplomatic isolation. There is no doubt that one long-term weakening factor has been the inability of her leaders to proclaim a clear policy on the Occupied Territories after the 1967 War. Even her friends blame her isolation on her own negative attitudes and accuse her of being reactive, of missing opportunities and foregoing useful relationships through lack of imagination. It could be said that she has for too long sought refuge in the intransigence of the weak, in a fortress-Israel mentality, when she has in fact outgrown that weakness.

On the other hand, it is possible to look at Israeli foreign policy in another light: to postulate that her political and military leaders have given profound thought to the question of national survival, both in the short term and in the long term; that between Dayan's 'creation of facts' and Begin's insistence on the sacred indivisibility of the Biblical Eretz Israel there is a hard-headed correspondence of vision. Confronted with Arab pressure, and in the teeth of the United States, she has single-mindedly continued to create facts. In the south she has achieved a secure frontier with Egypt. In the north-east, the Golan Heights, overlooking Damascus, have been annexed without further incident to

122

Israel. Operation Peace for Galilee has been a success in so far as it has disposed of the PLO as a military force and induced Yasser Arafat to consider coming to terms with King Hussein of Jordan. It is not surprising that the more hard-line Arab states should do their best to deter such an eventuality. If it were to come about that Jordan became the recognised territorial homeland for the Palestinians, and if, at the same time, Israel were already to have established enough of a presence in Judea and Samaria through a strategically placed chain of Jewish settlements, then she probably estimates that she would be able safely to concede an acceptable measure of administrative independence and economic well-being to the remaining Arab townships to make life tolerable. This scenario offers a fair prospect of Israel securing her long eastern frontier. There remains Syria in the north. Had Operation Peace for Galilee resulted in a relatively demilitarised Lebanon under the Israeli-groomed Bashir Gemayel, Israel's northern frontier problem would have been almost solved. Syria would have remained the intransigent arch-enemy, but the very presence of Soviet military backing in Syria, taken in conjunction with American support for Israel, might be calculated to curb Syria's military initiative. As it is, Israel is left with a very unstable Lebanese neighbour and no viable leader in sight there capable of taking control of the divided population.

If Israel has indeed been pursuing such a coherent pattern of foreign policy objectives, then she can claim a high success rate on the most important issues. But she must not complain if the losers and their friends occasionally call 'foul'. Neither must she or her diaspora lobby profess too much moral purity or the upholding of special human values. Success and survival must be their own reward and justification. Some Israelis are worried about the human cost of their government's policies, and because they now feel secure enough from the threat of annihilation to count the cost, some of them question both the ends and the means. It is for Israelis to judge.

124

Part II

MUBARAK'S EGYPT

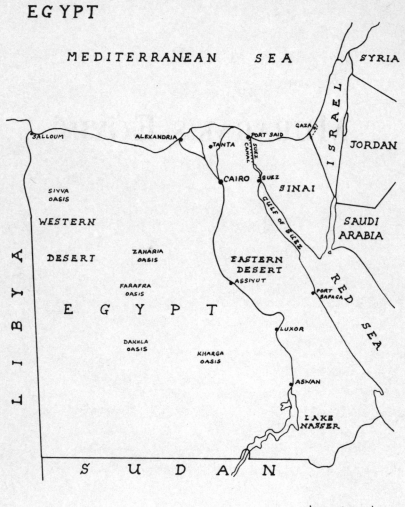

EGYPT

1

Before the Revolution: 1952

On 26 January 1952 the mob set fire to Cairo. By the end of that day 700 buildings had been gutted, more than 30 people killed and many others injured. It went down in the history of modern Egypt as 'Black Saturday'. Six months later, on 23 July, a small group of Army officers under General Neguib staged a *coup d'état* and took control of Cairo and then of Alexandria, where the King, Faruq, had retired for the summer with his Government. On 26 July the King boarded the royal yacht, *Mahrusa*, and sailed into exile to a 21-gun salute. It was not a bloody coup, but it marked a turning point in the development of modern Egypt and produced a new system of government which, so far, has brought successively Presidents Gamal Nasser, Anwar el-Sadat and Hosni Mubarak to supreme power in Egypt.

This opening chapter will look at the build-up of conflicting social, economic and political pressures that made the 1952 military coup seem to all parties concerned, both within Egypt and abroad, almost inevitable if not positively desirable. We shall see how the liberal democratic system of government under a constitutional monarchy, which had been imposed on Egypt earlier in the century by the British, had become incapable of producing a government which could control the bitterly divided and disillusioned political forces which the system itself had created, and how, by 1956, conditions in Egypt had become ripe for the emergence of an authoritarian, if not despotic régime.

To understand the social and political conditions prevailing in Egypt in 1952, one must understand the nature of the British connection, which started with British military occupation of the country in 1882, and the reasons for that occupation, which reach further back into Egyptian history.

Modern Egyptian history is usually dated from Napoleon's invasion in 1799. While the subsequent French occupation only lasted two years, it marked a turning point for Egypt. The conquering French forces brought with them new political and social ideas from a fermenting Europe and for the first time attracted European, including British, attention to the strategic value of the country. Napoleon swept away the Ottoman Turkish provincial administration which had ruled Egypt since 1517. Ottoman rule had been tacitly supported by Britain, with the object of maintaining a friendly power astride the overland route to India. So, in 1801, with British initiative, an Anglo-Turkish force was mustered to compel the French to withdraw. This inaugurated a period of British involvement in Egyptian affairs which lasted until 1956 and the so-called 'Suez Crisis'.

The destruction of the old corrupt Turkish administration by these French and British initiatives, left a local power vacuum which was soon filled by the leader of the Albanian contingent in the Anglo-Ottoman force, Muhammad Ali Pasha. Although he was not Egyptian but Albanian, he played a very important part in the early development of modern Egypt and dominated its national life for the first half of the nineteenth century. He was a great reformer: politically he could be described as a benevolent autocrat for he assumed total control of the power infrastructure in the country; economically, he created state monopolies of staple products such as cotton and wheat, and regulated the economy through these monopolies; militarily, he created a

128

very powerful army which began to adopt the techniques of modern European warfare, and which, in 1840, was able to advance through Palestine and Syria to the very borders of Turkey – the Ottoman–Turkish heartland – before being restrained and defeated by British and French sea-power. The military aspect of Ali Pasha's reforms was perhaps the most important, especially his realisation that only by imitating European methods of war did Egypt stand a chance of defending herself from later European domination. In fact the principal purpose of his political and financial measures was to create a sturdy state structure wherein he could build up a strong army.

The Napoleonic invasion had severed Egypt from Ottoman control in all but name. Although Muhammad Ali was still technically the Sultan's representative in Egypt, he effectively established a new Albanian dynasty there which survived until 1952. Yet despite its achievements this dynasty came to be despised and hated by Egyptians. When Muhammad Ali died in 1848, he left behind him an Egypt which was militarily and politically independent with a sound and expanding industrial base and administrative infrastructure. His ambitious modernisation projects, irrigation, road-building and expansion of economic activity, had only been achieved with the influx of a large number of European experts and advisers. They brought with them customs and attitudes which rubbed off on a growing Egyptian bourgeoisie, and over a few decades became a serious destabilising influence, as we shall see in a later chapter. Modernisation had also brought with it heavy debts which were to cause a national catastrophe forty years later and result in the loss of Muhammad Ali's hard-earned independence.

If Ali's successor had been as strong a character as his father, Egyptian history might well have taken a different course, for at that time there was no reason why, with sound management, Egypt could not have industrialised soon after

Europe. However, the series of relatives who succeeded him, Ibrahim, Abbas, Said and Ismail, were none of them capable of continuing his work. Said is remembered for the concession he granted in 1856 to the French engineer Ferdinand de Lesseps to build a canal through the Isthmus of Suez, a concession vehemently opposed by the British, who saw it as another French bid for domination of the sea-lanes to the Far East. Over the next one hundred years the canal, more than anything else, was to play a crucial part in Egypt's relations with Europe, and especially with Britain.

Most economic activity in Egypt at this time was the result of European investment projects which demanded financial returns. Under Ibrahim, Abbas and Said, the Egyptian financial system slipped into the hands of Europeans, and an already large bureaucracy expanded still further, while the land-owning class, which had been encouraged by Muhammad Ali, became wealthier and increasingly imitative of European life-styles and manners. Ismail Pasha, the grandson of Muhammad Ali, who succeeded in 1863, received the nickname 'the impatient Europeaniser'. Indeed, he was so enamoured of the new culture that he borrowed heavily abroad to finance extravagant European-style boulevards and public buildings in Cairo and Alexandria, as well as building bridges, roads and railways. It was under Ismail that the Egyptian Museum was founded and that Europeans became interested in Egyptology. He persuaded the Ottoman Sultan to grant him the title of Khedive and increase his powers to raise foreign debts. He soon affected the airs and graces of the most glamorous European monarchs, and boasted: 'My country is no longer in Africa, it is in Europe.' He was a talented and interesting character, but a disastrous ruler for Egypt at a crucial point in her history. Through Ismail's financial irresponsibility, during the period 1863 to 1875, Egypt became entirely subject to European financial creditors. By 1875, Ismail could no longer even afford to service the country's debts let alone

130

Israel's Prime Minister, Menachem Begin

David Ben Gurion reading the Declaration of Independence

Yitzhak Rabin and Golda Meir

Narkis, Dayan and Rabin entering Jerusalem in 1967

Shimon Peres

Gamal Nasser (Associated Press)

Sadat and Begin in Jerusalem

After the signing of the Camp David Agreements

Mubarak and Begin

President Hosni Mubarak of Egypt (Associated Press)

pay them off. He was obliged to sell off Egypt's share in the Suez Canal Company to Benjamin Disraeli, the British Prime Minister of the day, for the relatively paltry sum of £4,000,000; and even this merely put off the day of reckoning. Incidentally, Disraeli's purchase marks the true beginning of direct British involvement in Egyptian internal affairs, for Britain now had something valuable to lose, both financially and strategically, if the Egyptian economy collapsed and its monarchy crumbled.

The following year Ismail postponed repayment of debts to European investors. By this time financial weakness had so undermined his political position that he allowed Britain and France to impose on Egypt what was known as Dual Control. This involved a European Debt Commission which, through the administration of two Debt Controllers, one British and one French, was to oversee Egyptian economic activity and ensure that income from customs dues and excise went to her European creditors. It represented an almost total loss of financial sovereignty, and after the imposition of Dual Control, Ismail was increasingly looked upon by Egyptians as a stooge of the Europeans. There was an upsurge of anti-Khedive and anti-European feeling in the country. By 1879, both Britain and France were aware of a 'nationalist', xenophobic trend in Egyptian attitudes, and the British induced the Ottoman Sultan to depose Ismail, as a suitable scapegoat. This was not difficult, because ever since the Napoleonic invasion, the Ottoman Sultan had sought some way of forcing Egypt back to its old subservient provincial position before the French occupation.

Ismail was succeeded by his son, Tewfik, and for the next three years Egyptian internal affairs continued to deteriorate rapidly. Tewfik was a rather weak character, utterly unsuited to the historic role imposed upon him. He became the victim of increasing criticism from intellectuals, nationalists and landowners, for whom he represented the twin evils of foreign domination and autocratic palace government.

131

The British occupation of Egypt in 1882 was triggered by an uprising called the 'Orabi Revolt'. Orabi was an ordinary Egyptian soldier of peasant stock who made bold to present the Khedive with a petition from a group of soldiers for the remedy of certain grievances and for the dismissal of the unpopular Circassian Minister of War. (We shall see later how, at this time, nearly all the ministers and palace officials were not of native Egyptian stock.) Orabi was arrested, but was subsequently released by comrades-in-arms who broke up his court martial, arrested the military judges who were trying him, and then forced the Government to appoint Orabi Minister of War. An unlikely scenario, perhaps, which highlights two important points: first, the complete loss of credibility which the Khedive and his Government had suffered in the eyes of the general populace; secondly, and more importantly, it marked an ominous precedent in Egyptian national life – that armed force could be a successful weapon against an established political system and could achieve extraordinary results. Orabi embodied the revulsion felt by many Egyptians against a government which they felt had mortgaged the country to foreign financial and strategic interests, and he thereby became a popular 'nationalist' hero.

The European reaction, and especially that of the British was fear that if Orabi could succeed in causing massive 'nationalist' disaffection among the people, then it was possible that the whole Khedival political structure, together with its European-orientated financial arrangements, could be swept away, with consequent loss of control of the Suez Canal. By 1882 Orabi's agitation had turned into mob action in Cairo and Alexandria and there were incidents of looting and vandalising of foreign property. The Khedive was obliged to withdraw to Alexandria to be near the British fleet which had mustered off the coast. Something had to be done about 'Orabi Pasha'. In July 1882 the British fleet bombarded Orabist coastal fortifications and landed troops,

132

defeating the Orabist 'nationalists' at the battle of Tel el-Kebir. They then returned the Khedive to Cairo, together with a large British military garrison, while British troops effectively occupied the whole country.

The British occupation of Egypt in 1882 created untold problems for nearly one hundred years. She had invaded to defend the Khedival regime from certain defeat at the hands of a disorganised but popular Egyptian nationalist movement, which would not have honoured claims to financial compensation by foreign businesses and would have been an unstable and probably hostile force controlling a waterway of crucial imperial importance to Britain. Recurrently, from 1882 to 1956, Britain was to have great difficulty in justifying her presence in the country, and yet she could not contemplate withdrawal, and over the years this became a matter of national prestige. She did not declare Egypt a colony or even a protectorate until 1914 on the outbreak of the First World War, and this in itself bears witness to her dilemma: having occupied Egypt, Britain did not know what to do with it in the long term. In the short term her brief was clear: to put Egypt's finances in order. So, from 1883 until the outbreak of the First World War, Egypt was effectively ruled from the British Residency on the Nile in Cairo, in the name of a servile Khedive, by a succession of three 'British Agents and Consuls-General': Lord Cromer, Sir Eldon Gorst and Lord Kitchener.

Lord Cromer, known in Egypt, as el-Lurd, adopted an autocratic style of management and rarely left the Residency, but through meticulous planning and slow but methodical reconstruction, he restored Egypt to sound economic health by the turn of the century. While Egyptians held executive posts in government ministries, British advisers held total political control, and they derived their authority directly from British force of arms. While Cromer was undoubtedly an efficient and diligent administrator he paid no heed to the growing number of Egyptians who, while appreciative

133

of British success in rebuilding the economy, were becoming impatient for an opportunity to enter the political process and take some part in the decisions which affected their country. But Cromer was not a man to allow any group threatening total British control of affairs in Egypt to achieve national prominence. This was frustrating for the nationalists, who did not see why Britain was delaying the handing over to them of control of their own affairs. One thing Cromer did allow, from the highest motives, was the emergence of an indigenous press. This gradually became a forum for political debate, albeit restrained, and so it was that, although Cromer's term of office was one of strict political inaction, it was, nevertheless, a time of considerable political ferment.

From 1907 until 1911 Sir Eldon Gorst was British Agent. He was somewhat overshadowed by Cromer's reputation and faced increasing pressures from nationalists demanding a greater share in government. By 1911 it was felt that the deteriorating international situation in the Balkans and elsewhere called for a firm hand in Egypt, so the imposing Lord Kitchener was sent to Cairo. On the outbreak of war he was recalled to be Minister of War. At that point Sir John Maxwell, GOC British Forces in Egypt, imposed martial law on the country and declared that Britain would defend Egypt and bear the cost. In order to clarify the questionable legal position, Egypt was declared a British Protectorate. It was seen as little more than a legalisation of the status quo. It might have been expected that Egyptian nationalists would interpret this as a step towards outright annexation, and oppose it fiercely. In fact, it was seen as a positive step. For one thing it detached Egypt once and for all, legally, from the Ottoman Empire with which Britain was now at war. For another thing, it clarified the British position, which was now an official commitment to prepare Egypt for independence after the war.

During the First World War Egypt became a base for

British and imperial troops, and of major importance to the British war effort. Most Egyptians remained politically passive, waiting for the end of hostilities, when Britain would allow the country to take control of its own affairs and hand over to those Egyptian administrators she had been training for the past thirty years. National aspirations had coalesced into a National Party (as well as other groupings we shall look at later) under the leadership of Saad Zaglul, a man of peasant stock, like Orabi, who had been involved in politics since 1906, when he had been pro-British. Since then he had gradually become disillusioned and had joined the moderate nationalist faction, which was to play an important role in Egyptian affairs for the next forty years.

In 1919, at the Versailles Peace Conference, where the victorious powers decided how to allot the spoils of war, Britain and France carved the Middle East into two spheres of influence through a system of mandates. Syria and Lebanon went to France, Palestine to Britain. Britain had no wish to lose her position of total dominance in Egypt, which she had almost come to regard as a 'right'; and yet, having declared Egypt a Protectorate in 1914, she now had to take some steps to satisfy Egyptian public opinion without withdrawing her troops from the Canal Zone or losing her influence over internal affairs. Zaglul and his followers naturally demanded to be allowed to attend the Peace Conference as representatives of the Egyptians. The British, however, refused him permission to go. It would have been intolerable to have had him in an international forum demanding complete independence and British withdrawal. Instead, they invited die-hard pro-British Egyptian politicians who had little public support, but who, because they held land and status under British rule, could be counted on to support a pro-British line. Zaglul's answer to this was to whip up agitation in the towns and countryside for a delegation that would put true Egyptian demands before the world. His campaign was highly successful and the movement which grew out of it came to be known as the Wafd (delegation). The British, feeling their position was being eroded by nationalist hotheads, deported Zaglul first to Aden and then to the Seychelles. Within Egypt, however, the Wafd had become a major popular movement whose main political planks were simple enough for any Egyptian to identify with: namely total British withdrawal and a declaration of independence.

Before long the British found difficulty in locating any public figures who were prepared to settle in public for anything less than British withdrawal and independence. So, in 1922, after serious civil disturbances and a Commission of Enquiry, the British bowed to the inevitable and at the same time rescued what chestnuts they could out of the fire. On 15 March they unilaterally declared Egypt independent, with four Reserved Points which were to remain under absolute British control, subject to negotiation at a later date: these four were the security of imperial communications in Egypt, the defence of Egypt against foreign aggression, the protection of foreign interests and minorities in the country, and the territory of the Sudan. These Reserved Points were to become the focus of anti-British agitation in Egypt until the Second World War, and they will be looked at in much more detail in the chapter on politics.

In the shadow of the chronic problem of Anglo-Egyptian relations, Egypt was torn by another profound internal struggle during the inter-war years. When Britain had declared Egypt a Protectorate, this had changed the status of the Khedive to that of Sultan, thereby emphasising the break with the Ottoman Sultanate. In 1922, the Declaration of Independence named Sultan Fuad King Fuad I of Egypt, and while no provision was made in the Declaration as to the form of government to be adopted, it was assumed that it would follow the British pattern of a constitutional monarchy. The inter-war experiment in parliamentary

136

government was dominated by three forces which eventually combined to undermine and overthrow it. The three forces were first, the Wafd party, which proceeded to win massive majorities in all parliamentary elections and then to make unacceptable demands on the British for concessions on the Reserved Points; secondly, the British, who were anxious to create a constitutional parliamentary democracy in Egypt, but at the same time needed to ensure there was a Parliament which would not make excessively nationalist demands; and thirdly, the King, who was regarded with extreme suspicion by the Wafd, for he could dissolve Parliament indefinitely and appoint his own Prime Minister (which he frequently did). In fact he deliberately used the powers granted him under the 1923 constitution to further his ambitions and concentrate power in his own hands. He came to be viewed with distaste by almost all parliamentarians, who felt that his contemptuous treatment of the elected chamber enabled the British to have the final say in Egyptian political life, since a British force of arms was the ultimate basis of the King's authority. When the King, or the British, felt the Wafd was becoming too powerful and likely to enact laws which might undermine either of their respective positions in the country, the King would dissolve Parliament, postpone elections, and appoint one of his loyal palace politicians, such as his Chamberlain, as Prime Minister. Eventually pressure from the Wafd and the populace, or, on at least one occasion, from the British, would force the King to call elections, and this would again produce a Parliament dominated by the Wafd.

The Wafd party, led by Zaglul until his death in 1927, and thereafter by Nahas, was not itself blameless of the abuse of power. Its leaders did not hesitate to make full use of their overwhelming majority in Parliament to enact restrictive laws of association and press regulations, and to bestow political patronage on their supporters. They tended to regard the weak and fragmented parliamentary opposition

137

as renegades and political outcasts, rather than as a healthy source of criticism and encouragement in dealing with the British and the King. The combination of a power-hungry monarch and a political party that regarded electoral victory as a licence to trample its opponents underfoot, did not present an encouraging spectacle of parliamentary democracy.

In 1930 King Fuad dissolved Parliament and appointed his own men, first Ismail Sidqi and then Fattah Yahia, to lead Governments which remained in power without parliamentary endorsement until 1935. It was a critical period, because during those years, with public and constitutional political activity monopolised by palace appointees bent on subverting the parliamentary system, the Wafd and the smaller parties came to the conclusion that they had no alternative but to resort to extra-parliamentary activities such as demonstrations, unofficial congresses, etc.

By 1935, as these pressures built up, the British became increasingly anxious to see a constitutionally elected Parliament exercising real power in Egypt, and were prepared to see this come about at the expense of the King. However, the overriding factor in the British calculations was the Italian invasion of Abyssinia in 1935, followed by annexation the following year. Where, hitherto, Britain had been happy to stand on the side-lines, acting only as the referee of last resort, she now perceived a major threat to her position in Africa, and, as history would bear out, to her global imperial interests. Egypt's strategic position astride the Suez Canal was to prove vital to Britain's success in the war against Nazi Germany and in maintaining her ascendancy in the Eastern Mediterranean. If Anglo-Egyptian relations were to be put to the test of another war, Britain felt it expedient to extend an olive branch of sorts: she agreed to renegotiate the terms of the 1922 Declaration of Independence and its Reserved Points. She felt that a treaty concluded with a constitutional and representative government stood a better chance of holding than one negotiated with an unpopular monarch. Britain was to withdraw to a garrison in the Suez Canal Zone, Egypt was to be free to appoint its own diplomats abroad, the British High Commissioner became His Majesty's Ambassador to Egypt, and an Egyptian replaced the British Inspector General of the Egyptian Army. Egypt also became a member of the League of Nations in 1937.

Obviously these were cosmetic changes, but they temporarily mollified most Egyptian politicians, who were as concerned as the British at the turn events were taking in Africa and Europe. It was seen by the Wafd as a step in the right direction, which was certainly true from their point of view since it amounted to British support in returning the Wafd to power against the wishes of the King. As we shall see, however, some young Egyptians were actively working for the Axis powers, on the understanding that a British defeat would mean freedom from British domination.

In 1937 King Fuad was succeeded by Farouk, who had been Regent since 1936. Faruq was an exceptionally weak and pusillanimous man who, like Ismail before him, was badly cast in his historic role, a key figure in bringing about the collapse of the system upon which his authority was based. He was to be ignominiously exiled in 1952. In the meantime, he was adept at using the techniques his father had used to bolster his own position at the expense of Parliament.

In the autumn of 1937 the Wafd was once again forced out of office by the King and a 'palace' Government was formed under Ali Maher, considered a 'King's man'. Excluded from power, a substantial section of the Wafd and of public opinion sympathised with the Axis powers. Their ideology of a disciplined, paramilitary regime was considered by many people to be better suited to Egypt than liberal democracy, which merely prolonged British domination.

On the outbreak of war in September 1939, Egypt severed diplomatic relations with Germany but did not declare war.

The British had grave suspicions about the pro-Axis sympathies of the Prime Minister, Ali Maher, and of King Farouk, but were prepared to tolerate them for the time being. In the 'dark days' of 1942, when Rommel was advancing across the Western Desert towards the Egyptian border at Salloum (which they later occupied, but they were driven back at the Battle of El-Alamein), a national drama was to ensue; but by this time Maher's successor, Hasanayn, had collapsed dead in Parliament and had been succeeded in his turn by yet another 'King's man', Sirry. In the face of civil unrest, Sirry was having difficulty remaining in power. There was a national food crisis and popular resentment was mainly directed at the government of the day. The British ambassador in 1942 was Sir Miles Lampsom (later Lord Killearn), and he, fully aware of the implications for Britain of military defeat in Egypt, took the most drastic measures available to him. On the afternoon of 4 February 1942 British tanks surrounded the Abdin Palace, Farouk's official residence in Cairo, and Lampson, escorted by a posse of armed guards, marched into Farouk's study and handed him a note which demanded that he ask Nahas, the Wafd leader, to form a government or face the consequences (i.e. abdication). Farouk gave way, but the incident went down in history as the 'February 4th incident', and, as we shall see, it was to have dire repercussions for the British. It shows that in the opinion of the British, Nahas was the only man capable of forming a government that would not rebel (at least in the immediate future) against the British, and which would be able to keep the peace until the end of the war. However high-handed the British action might seem in retrospect, in 1942 Britain was by no means certain of winning the war, and she presumably felt that wartime considerations overruled what was, on the face of it, gross interference in Egypt's internal affairs.

By 1945 the Egyptians were ready for a final showdown with the British. Peace was restored, and they demanded complete withdrawal of British troops, at least from the cities where they had been deployed during the war. The British, for their part, needed to come to terms with a new set of post-war realities in Anglo-Egyptian relations. They cannot be said to have handled the situation with much delicacy. The years 1945 to 1952 were a period of intense political ferment and of growing disillusionment with the British and the whole system of government which had come to be associated with them. The international power vacuum created by the defeat of Germany and Japan was swiftly filled by the United States and the Soviet Union, competing for influence in Europe and elsewhere. By 1947 the cold war had already begun and was to freeze further during the following ten years. It is important to bear in mind that the 1952 revolution and its aftermath in Egypt were set against this background of cold war rivalry. The general spirit of superpower competition and international upheaval was a destabilising influence on Egyptian political life. Faruq, with his scandalous private life and blatant display of arbitrary power, turned the whole institution of the monarchy into an object of hatred and loathing for all but the wealthiest landowners and courtiers who benefited from the system he embodied and protected.

Generally, speaking, in 1945, Egyptians were searching for a new post-war path to progress, in much the same spirit as the British when they voted a Labour Government into power. But the Egyptians saw a major stumbling block to the future happiness and prosperity of their country – continued British presence in their cities and in the Canal Zone. Once this problem was eliminated, other internal problems could, with time, be sorted out. This was, of course, a simplistic attitude, since the underlying discontent really stemmed more from disillusionment with the bankrupt internal constitutional set-up. People asked why, in the inter-war period, it had failed to bring true independence and social justice to the country, and why they had wasted precious years in

141

bitter struggles between King and Parliament, and allowed the British to perpetuate their influence through a policy of divide-and-rule.

In 1945, then, the Wafdist Prime Minister Nuqrashi (Nahas had died in 1942), reflecting this new national mood, demanded that the British re-negotiate the 1936 Treaty. Such negotiations, he said, must this time result in a British commitment to total withdrawal from all bases in Egypt. Britain, however, seeing herself in a world context, was in no mood to negotiate. She felt she was now confronting the Soviet Union across Europe and that any withdrawal from so strategic an area as the Suez Canal at such a juncture was out of the question. As Anglo-Egyptian discussions dragged on, so Egyptian resentment grew, and by 1948 a new factor had entered the equation. A Jewish state declared its independence in part of Palestine, under what the Egyptians saw as British auspices. In fact Britain merely declared her intention of leaving Palestine, and handed the question of Arab-Jewish relations in the area over to the United Nations, which voted for partition into two separate states, one Jewish, one Arab. The two sides were left to fight it out on the ground. On 14 May 1948, the day Israel declared her independence, the Egyptian Army crossed the southern border and headed towards Tel Aviv and Jerusalem.

By early 1949, the newly formed Israeli Defence Force had secured a front line around the Gaza Strip and along the southern border of old Palestine to Eilat and the Red Sea. These frontiers were subsequently confirmed by an Armistice Agreement signed in Rhodes that year.

The effect of this defeat (for this is what it was) for the Egyptian Army at the hands of 'Israelis' who were reported to have been fighting against odds of up to seventy to one was really the final blow to the *ancien régime*. There were bitter recriminations among Army officers who accused the King and politicians of profiteering and supplying inferior equipment to the Army. Whatever the foundations of these

142

accusations, the incontrovertible fact is that from the defeat in 1948 to the overthrow of the régime in 1952, events marched along an unstoppable course. Street demonstrations by Nuqrashi's Wafd supporters developed into attacks on British property and personnel, which the British saw as virtually sponsored by the Wafd Government itself. They protested, but such was the pressure put on Nuqrashi that he resigned. By now events had overwhelmed the politicians and there were very few with the national stature to take control. Eventually Sidqi, the ageing Prime Minister of the 1930s' 'palace' Government, who was nationally respected, if not liked, took over and clamped down strongly on the protestors. The demonstrations burnt themselves out.

By this time the British were seriously concerned that Egypt was becoming ungovernable under the existing political arrangements. A conciliatory message from Prime Minister Atlee in London referred to Britain and Egypt as 'equal partners having interests in common'. Yet Britain still retained considerable military forces in the country; garrisons in the major cities and a huge base in the Canal Zone. In 1949, as a 'concession', the British agreed to withdraw from the cities to the Canal Zone. But the gesture came too late. The Wafd, under Nuqrashi, continued to agitate for total British withdrawal.

By 1951, the Wafd was being carried along by public opinion disillusioned with their impotent politicians, with their hated King, and with the British who had become national bogeymen. Disturbances continued, and Sidqi resigned out of desperation with the Wafd and its tactics. Nuqrashi came back, but he soon realised that the agitation had become nationwide disaffection, and that, even as leader of the Wafd, he could not control it. By now the British were so alarmed at the prospect of anarchy in Egypt that they withdrew totally to the Canal Zone garrison and made conciliatory noises. However, by this time not even a complete withdrawal of British forces from the Canal Zone itself would have defused the impending crisis.

On 26 January 1952 the mob set fire to Cairo. Six months later a small group of Army officers under General Neguib, staged a *coup d'état* and sent Farouk into exile. The old actors had been hissed off the stage. But the new cast of officers who took over from them had no clear idea what to put in its place. The man who would chart a new course for Egypt was one of this new cast, Gamal Nasser.

2

The Political Background 1952–83

Nasser, at the height of his power, was military leader, political leader, and vital embodiment of the nation. We propose to try to clarify a complex and volatile set of circumstances and identify factors reaching back into the nineteenth century to events outlined in chapter 1. This, it is hoped, will make them more comprehensible in the forms manifested in the last thirty years.

One factor was the urban élite, the commercial middle-class. It began to grow under Muhammad Ali, whose reforming zeal changed the face of the country in the first half of the nineteenth century. As a manager of Egyptian affairs he was unrivalled by his successors until the rise of Nasser. But his political centralisation produced a top-heavy bureaucracy which has inhibited efficient administration ever since. Europeans imported into Egypt to help to implement Muhammad Ali's agricultural and industrial plans eventually trained an indigenous Egyptian class of professional engineers, lawyers, bankers and teachers, all vital to good administration in a developing country, and these became a new European-educated urban élite. The word is used deliberately with its overtones of separateness and perceived superiority. While, in the early years, this class was totally loyal to the ruler, later the seeds of discontent began to grow. They, who were learning how to manage the country's affairs, began to look more critically at the ruler who contin-

145

ued to assert that he alone had an absolute right to manage them.

Another factor was the Consultative Assembly, which the Khedive set up in 1866 in order to enter into a dialogue with this new urban middle-class. It did not meet often, and its members were not elected but appointed by the Khedive himself; nevertheless, it gradually assumed the attributes of a representative body. Although it in no way represented the interests of any Egyptians outside the narrow class to which its members belonged, it did express the aspirations of a broad section of the people to free themselves from foreign domination. Yet this same élite social group felt a sense of relief when the British stepped in after 1882 to restore the country's financial affairs to health, their resentment at foreign intervention being largely outweighed by their sense of common interest. They also saw rosy prospects in the fact that Egyptians were to be trained to take over the British role in the foreseeable future. They were the chief beneficiaries of the growth of a free press at the turn of the century, and it was they who began to discuss new political ideas and ideologies and the role of religion in their evolving society. A traditional Islamic society was trying to find a response to the challenge posed by European ideas.

It was not only in Egypt that this was happening. Similar movements were growing up among Muslims in Central Asia and North Africa. In Egypt, however, discussion centred on how best to reform Islamic society in order to resist the perceived European threat. There were three lines of thought about what should be done. Some people believed that society should be reformed along stricter Islamic lines and that the reason it had become so fragmented was because it had deviated from the true ideals of Islam. A second group believed that Islam itself should be reformed to conform to the modern realities of government and power. A third group held that once Egypt had rid herself of the corrupting force of the British, she should pursue her own Islamic path. All three groups were agreed on the imperative need for British withdrawal. That was the common ground on which the twentieth-century parties superimposed their individual priorities. Muslims right across the political spectrum were attracted by the Wafd and its unspecific nationalism, and it was this party which, with the King, dominated the parliamentary scene.

Certain groups did not participate in the parliamentary system. One of these, the Muslim Brotherhood, was the more fundamentalist wing of Islam in the country. It called for a return to the golden age of Islam, and was opposed to corruption, both 'external' in the form of British influence, and 'internal' in the form of the King and the national politicians. The Brotherhood's activities focused on violent, populist action, and in view of this it was prevented by the British and by the King from putting up parliamentary candidates. Thus it was obliged to establish an extra-parliamentary organisation. It drew support from all levels of society.

An Egyptian Communist party maintained a small but steady membership after its foundation in 1922, but these were mainly intellectuals and members of minority groups, especially Jews and Copts. Communism was regarded as a foreign, godless ideology, alien to such a deeply traditional and religious society and irrelevant to Egypt's needs and conditions. It had no great political significance.

In 1933 a paramilitary movement was founded, called Young Egypt (Misr al-Fatat). It was modelled on the fascist movements of Central Europe and it also had a tough section, the Green Shirts. It made similar nationalist demands to the Muslim Brotherhood, but it did not see reform in the totally Islamic terms of the Brotherhood, laying more emphasis on straightforward Egyptian nationalism. The movement was suppressed during the Second World War owing to its strong pro-Axis sympathies.

The British must take some blame for the weakening of the

parliamentary system, because, by undermining its ability to act in the one policy area where it would have commanded popular confidence, namely relations with the British themselves, they had strengthened support for movements outside Parliament. After the Second World War the pressures outside became overwhelming and the fragile parliamentary system collapsed into political anarchy. During the years between the end of the war and the revolutionary coup of 1952, the regime can be said to have lost the confidence of practically the entire population. Not even the would-be reformers had any clear plans for restoring political viability or even a tolerable degree of public order. In an attempt to gain the support of more radical groups, the Wafd even gave them weapons to fight the British in the Canal Zone, but more often than not these were used against other Egyptians, and the proliferation of arms only served to further destabilise the situation. Egypt was in a pre-revolutionary state.

Where did Gamal Abd-el Nasser come from and what qualities and circumstances set him at the head of his generation? He was born in 1918 in a village in Upper Egypt not far from Alexandria, the son of a post-office clerk. From the age of seven he was brought up by an uncle in Cairo. He grew up, therefore, in the lower ranks of the urban middle-class which, through education and gravitation to the big cities, managed to achieve some measure of social mobility. But he never entirely lost the awareness of his roots in the countryside and this gave him a broader understanding of both sections of the population, their problems and also what stirred their hearts and minds. The formative years of fifteen to eighteen he spent at school in Cairo during the period when the capital was seething with social and political ferment. Record has it that he was a thoughtful, introspective young man who explored all the conflicting ideologies circulating at the time. Like most young Egyptians of his

148

generation he nursed a vehement hatred of the British. He became a student of law. However, when, in 1936, the Military Academy at Abbasiya opened the officer corps to Egyptians of all classes, he signed up as a cadet. He was then eighteen. He found himself one of a self-selected élite group, the first generation of officers from the new expanded intake. And of this élite group, later to become the so-called Free Officers, Nasser became the recognised leader.

It was, as we have seen, the Palestine War of 1948 which gave the impetus to the formation of the Free Officers' cabal. Nasser himself fought in Palestine and saw action at Falluja, in the Negev, where he was wounded, in company with several other Free-Officers-to-be, in a successful holding operation against Israeli forces. The war left him with very bitter feelings about the British, the King and the whole corrupt, inefficient régime, and he returned to Cairo determined to change the course of Egyptian history. He was not really a complicated character. Essentially he was driven by the conviction that Egypt needed a new leader and that he was that leader. He saw himself as a true native-born Egyptian, untainted by wealth or foreign influence. He was not a man to take account of the subtler corruption of power itself. As he saw it, the Army was the only group in the country capable of altering the status quo. The politicians had kowtowed first to the British, then to the King, and were to be blamed for the relatively poor performance of the Egyptian Army in the war (relative, that is, to the Jewish forces). Smarting under the humiliation of the war, the Free Officers were only too receptive to rumours that the British, together with the King, had sabotaged an Egyptian victory in the interests of protecting the Zionist settlers in Palestine, thereby permitting them to establish an independent state of Israel. In the wake of the defeat, the Free Officers began to recruit increasing numbers into their secret society. They organised a cell system which succeeded in evading detection right up to the moment of action.

149

The coup took place on 25 June 1952. It was effected without bloodshed; no shots were fired. The King was out of the way in Alexandria. The Free Officers simply took over the military headquarters in Cairo, unopposed, and the broadcasting station, from which the change of régime was announced to the people and to the world. There were no street demonstrations; in fact the riots which had been a feature of the deteriorating pre-revolutionary situation, died down. The coup took place entirely inside the Army. Whereas the old military cadres had placed themselves under the impotent political arm of the state, the new cadres were asserting the reality of their power over those same politicians. Nasser saw the coup as merely one step in an historic sequence of events. As such, it was carefully planned and efficiently though circumspectly carried out.

When Nasser and the Free Officers carried out their coup they did so in the name of the Egyptian people and with the avowed purpose of ridding the country of the 'foreign' tyrant, King Farouk. Farouk had become the symbol of the *ancien régime* and even most of his own court were glad to see him removed. This action in itself gave the Free Officers a cloak of popular legitimacy. Moreover, in the days immediately following on the revolution, they stood discreetly in the shadow of the respected figure of General Muhammad Neguib.

Neguib was some twenty years older than Nasser's group, and the public saw him as a solid, honest general who had reluctantly taken over the reins of power because it was the only means of ridding the nation of the tyrant King. They assumed, as Neguib himself probably did, that he would merely preside over a military interregnum to protect the country from the danger of civil war, after which the Army would return to barracks and the country would revert to a cleansed parliamentary democracy. This was the assumption of politicians like Nahas, the Wafd leader, and Ali Maher, the veteran palace Prime Minister. And so, for six months

150

after the coup, the junta of officers flirted with the pre-revolutionary parties.

The fact is they needed time. They were very inexperienced in the exercise of power, and they needed to test the political ground and get the feel of the popular national temper. But their indecision was not fundamental. There is no doubt that their intentions were deeply rooted and fixed from the start. Nasser and his friends sought undisputed power, and they sought it for a purpose so enormous (the transformation of Egypt, no less) that nothing less than totalitarian power would meet their needs. This was not, however, something that they proclaimed from the rooftops.

After a few months, when it became evident that the Free Officers did not intend to stand down, but were, on the contrary, seeking to consolidate their grip, there was widespread uneasiness in many sectors of the population. The Wafd, with its roots in the liberal tradition of Western Europe, maintained a commitment to parliamentary democracy. The extremist parties, of both left and right, despised Parliament and parliamentarians, but were not necessarily reassured by a military junta. The Muslim Brotherhood was openly hostile, and even within the armed forces the Free Officers had made inevitable enemies. They were constrained to advance with caution towards their goal.

A Revolutionary Command Council was set up. It was to rule by decree for a period of three years pending preparations for a new and democratic régime. In June 1953 the monarchy was abolished by decree and General Neguib made President of the Republic. Nasser became head of the executive, Abdul Hakim Amer Commander-in-Chief of the Armed Forces, and other Free Officers assumed important posts in the new administration. Gradually, under Nasser's leadership, the Free Officers established themselves. There was, however, still no political infrastructure in the country to underpin their régime.

The old political parties began to murmur against the Free

Officers. Not for long. They were formally dissolved and their property and assets confiscated. The Liberation Rally replaced all other political associations. It was not intended that the Rally should express any views independently of the Revolutionary Command Council; its function was to harness popular support. Within the RCC an inevitable power struggle developed, which culminated, in February 1954, in the resignation of Neguib. The path was now clear for Nasser to step into first place.

The transformation was now complete from the shadowy conspiratorial Nasser of June 1952 into the charismatic natural leader of Egypt two years later. His 'miraculous' escape from assassination on October 1954 at the hands of the Muslim Brotherhood, endowed him with supernatural qualities in the popular imagination; to criticise Nasser, the embodiment of the Egyptian revolution, became tantamount to criticising Egypt herself. In 1956 the legal niceties of this consolidation of power were completed. In January that year a new constitution was drawn up by Nasser and ratified by referendum (99.9 per cent). It established an exceptionally strong model of presidential government wherein Ministers were responsible, not to the elected assembly but to the President, who could dissolve the assembly and appoint and dismiss Ministers at will. A new era had begun. Nasser's personal autocracy was to remain unchallenged until after the national defeat of the 1967 War with Israel.

The Liberation Rally soon became redundant, having served its purpose of providing an alternative political focus during the initial years of confrontation with the remnants of the old liberal order. Both it and the RCC were replaced, in 1956, by the National Union. This, said Nasser, was to be the instrument through which 'the people could realise the aims of the revolution' – by which he meant his own aims. It was designed to give the stamp of legitimacy to his policies. As a legislature it was virtually impotent. Moreover, all the candidates were rigorously screened and called upon to pay a substantial deposit, which effectively excluded workers and peasants from standing. Its sole *raison d'être* was to rally loyal support for Nasser.

This brings us to the crux of Nasser's problem at this time. He had unlimited executive power and a co-operative, sycophantic, legislature, yet he had no clear idea of how to proceed with his grand designs. Restructuring society is a slow, painstaking business; land reform, the redistribution of wealth, clearing urban slums, the expansion of food production, and laying a sound basis for industrial development – all these produce social tensions, while they bear fruits only in the long term. Dictators are perennially faced with the need to justify their power. Yet Nasser had no ideology to motivate his people, his Army or even his oligarchy of close supporters. He fell back on the old pre-revolutionary rallying cry: Out with the British. In 1956 he nationalised the Suez Canal. Apart from the personal pleasure he must have derived from that stroke, he could bank on its popularity throughout the country. However doubtful the military glory of some aspects of the Suez War, if Nasser's first priority had been to take Britain down a peg, then that object was achieved.

With his position inside the country unassailable, Nasser turned to the possibilities of extending his power and influence beyond the boundaries of Egypt. He was still seeking a cause, an ideology, and he grasped at the nebulous concept of Arab unity. Whatever name one puts to Arab nationalism, it is merely an ideology, no more, since the so-called Arab World is fragmented, and its parts are at widely differing stages of political and cultural development. Egypt could, it was true, lay some just claim to leadership of this chimeric entity, for it was the largest and the most populous Arab state. It had a long cultural heritage and the most famous Muslim university, the Al-Azhar, in Cairo. Egypt would be the natural centre of an Arab Union. This would not only bolster up Nasser's position at home, but it would also provide an ideological platform from which to attack the existence of Israel, the intruder into the Arab World, the affront to Arab Unity in the region. Lastly, the concept appealed to Nasser's desire for self-aggrandisement. It will need a greater, wiser, more comprehensive man than Nasser to transform a country of the size and complexity of Egypt. He fell back on simpler concepts like national pride and the chess-board power politics of national alliances and military ventures.

Egypt's three-year-long political union with Syria between 1958 and 1961 is a case in point. Nasser's motives for seeking the creation of a United Arab Republic were straightforward; promotion of the concept of Arab unity and pursuit of a potential military stranglehold on the arch-enemy Israel. Egypt was the stronger partner. The Syrian position was more complex, and here the key to the situation was the Ba'ath (Renaissance) party. Formed in the late 1940s by Michel Aflaq and Saleh Bitar as a focus for Arab nationalist sentiment in the wake of independence from France, it proclaimed the essential unity of all those residents of Arab countries who spoke Arabic. Language not the Muslim religion was the unifying factor. The Ba'ath party quickly grew in strength, because it was recognised that Arab unity, and its political expression, Arab nationalism, gave a country like Syria broader backing in her struggle against foreign domination, which they did not feel had disappeared with the official ending of the French Mandate. It also furnished them with a clear justification for attacking Israel. The mere impotent sense of injustice in the face of the *fait accompli* perpetrated in 1948 had proved to be a somewhat muted battle cry. Nevertheless, it may still seem a little strange that an independent state, with its own army and viable institutions, should even have considered entering into a political union with another state, let alone with a country dominated by an autocratic leader. The fact is, left-wing groups, including Communists, had secured a grip on the

154

Ba'ath party and even on a section of the Army, and the Government saw Egyptian intervention as perhaps the only way of averting a left-wing army coup. President Shukri Quatly was a conservative politician, cast in the mould of the pre-revolutionary Wafd leader, Nahas, and Arab unity, including by implication unity with another Arab country like Egypt, was, after all, a major tenet in the Ba'ath programme. It could be said that Nasser's Egypt had the power, while Ba'athist Syria had the ideology Nasser was seeking.

Nasser's terms for the union were characteristically uncompromising: all Syrian political parties were abolished and the Syrian Army was to play no part in politics. Egypt and Syria became the northern and southern regions of the United Arab Republic and Nasser was its President. However, after the initial enthusiasm had died down, the Syrians quickly came to resent Nasser's high-handed rule from Cairo. Syria was governed by Egyptians, and political and military morale fell to new depths. Nasser sent his old Free Officer friend Abdul Hakim Amer to try to pacify the frustrated Syrian public, but without success. Eventually resentment reached such a pitch that, on 28 September 1961, Syrian Army units marched on Damascus and staged a national uprising against Nasser's rule.

Nasser found himself in a tricky position. Arab unity was his avowed aim, but he had been incapable even of holding together two Arab countries within the UAR. He had staked a measure of his legitimacy both at home and abroad on the success of the UAR, and its collapse was a blow that seriously weakened his political position. The collapse actually represented a military defeat in so far as he had not been able to prevent Syrian secession by military means. His reaction was, perhaps, characteristic: the concept of Arab Unity had been sound, he argued; it was simply its application which had been wrong. 'It is imperative,' he said firmly, 'that we should now carry out a complete reform operation that will

155

reshape the ideals and morals of our society.' Instead of high-sounding platitudes he badly needed a new concrete political initiative to efface the failure. But his reaction was the straightforward one of the professional soldier: he sent troops to Yemen to support the republican side in the civil war there. The intention was to restore public confidence in the Army, and perhaps the Army's confidence in itself. It was a mistake. It dragged on for three years with disastrous long-term consequences. The war is dealt with in the next chapter.

On the home front, disappointed with Arab nationalism, he concentrated on Egyptian nationalism, over which he had at least some control. Yet although he had such an astute conception of power, he did not match this with a comparable political sense. Ten years after the Free Officers' coup he was still looking for some ideological justification for the revolution to supersede the original aim of ridding the country of a corrupt régime and a humiliating foreign occupation.

In 1962 Nasser drew up a Charter for National Action. This created a National Assembly and a new political body called the Arab Socialist Union. The ASU was to be the organ for the expression of the views of the masses. The new ideology which was to find expression through the ASU was defined as 'scientific socialism', and subsequently as 'Arab socialism'. Old-fashioned Western liberals might be under the impression that public opinion is a more or less spontaneous phenomenon and they might be puzzled at the notion of defining the colour of public opinion in the same breath as creating an organ for its notionally free expression. They live in a sheltered world. Initially it was Nasser's intention that the ASU should be something more than a mere rubber-stamp. It was to have its own Supreme Executive Committee, of which President Nasser was the Chairman. Ultimately, and foreseeably, the ASU degenerated into an updated version of the Liberation Rally, an instrument for

156

rousing and relaying popular support for the Chairman's policies. It did not constitute a viable alternative focus of authority for the populace, whose lives continued to be run by the traditional grass-roots system of village headsmen. No middle ground had been established. The Secretary General of the ASU was Ali Sabri, later to fall victim to Sadat's purge after Nasser's death. Sabri described the ASU as an organisation designed to provide 'proper guidance to the masses' – hardly a definition of a representative assembly.

The other body created by the Charter for National Action was the National Assembly. Ostensibly its function was to be the scrutiny and criticism of the actions of the executive. To this end it was nominally empowered to censure Ministers and even to call for their resignation. In fact the President could dissolve the National Assembly at his pleasure without giving any reason – presumably if it sought to exercise its power over the executive. The Speaker of the National Assembly was Anwar el Sadat. Other one-time Free Officers were also still strategically placed within the web of supreme power. Scientific socialism and Arab socialism soon coalesced to become Nasser's brand of Egyptian nationalism. When, in 1965, pressure began to mount for a withdrawal of Egyptian troops from the fruitless war in the Yemen, it was not through the ASU that public opinion made itself felt, but outside.

The catastrophic defeat of Egypt at the hands of Israel in 1967 was a far greater humiliation even than the secession of Syria from the UAR in 1961, if only because it was a military débâcle and Egyptian territory was actually lost to a foreign power. Nasser's reaction now, however, was similar to that in 1961. He blamed the implementation of the idea, namely the generals' conduct in the war, rather than the idea behind it, namely his own ambition to destroy Israel. This time he had to find some way to neutralise not only

157

political criticism of his leadership, but also criticism of the Army on which his power ultimately rested. In the first instance he resigned as President of the Republic, though he had no hesitation in allowing himself to be called back into office by popular acclaim. How else were the mass of the people to react? For most of them Nasser *was* Egypt, and for him to resign might well have precipitated a total collapse of the régime. What hand Nasser had in the demonstrations of solidarity is open to speculation. At all events, he was constrained to remain President. Through the media he explained to them that, to stand up to the new challenge – Israel – a new social order was needed. Arab unity had failed in 1961. Socialism, whether Arab, scientific or otherwise, had failed in 1967. Yet still a new national order failed to materialise.

Evidently Nasser lacked the creative imagination and the social commitment to bring it about, and his presence excluded the possibility of any other public figure securing the means to do so. His reaction to the events of 1967 was narrow and uninspired. On the political front he sponsored the Khartoum resolution which proclaimed: No recognition (of Israel), no peace and no negotiation. This was making the best of a bad job, since at that time no Arab state had a military option, and world opinion was on the side of Israel, who was regarded as the gallant victim whose pre-emptive strike was made only in the face of undisguised belligerency from all her neighbours, and especially Egypt. On the military front he made a scapegoat of his old friend Abdul Hakim Amer who had commanded the Egyptian forces during the war. Nasser instigated a press campaign against Amer who, in true Roman fashion, committed suicide. This was a two-fold tragedy, since in him Nasser lost not only an excellent general but the only man he trusted, and one who would have been a valuable source of support in the ensuing years.

Nasser never quite recovered his old credibility after the

158

1967 defeat. He had been the natural figurehead of the country, so Egypt's defeat had been his defeat. It had brought discredit on her chief arms supplier, the Soviet Union, and cooled relations between the two countries; yet recent events precluded her from turning to the West, either for trade or sympathy. He started to make concessions at home. In 1968 he set about refurbishing the ASU. He curbed the activities of the hated secret police and the intelligence service. He allowed more freedom to the student unions, who had always quietly despised his style of government; but far from being appeased they became involved in increasingly violent confrontations with the police and even with the Army. After fifteen years of repression there was a great yearning for greater freedom of expression. Nasser recognised the national mood. But the more concessions he made, the more vulnerable he made himself. With the relative decline in Nasser's power so there came a relative resurgence of opposition groups, especially the Muslim Brotherhood. Islamic revivalism in many parts of the Arab World started to make itself felt around 1967. The mould was cracking.

Nasser was a charismatic leader, something of a demagogue, but not a tyrant. In principle, he wanted to rouse the people and lead them, but not necessarily to repress. The large and cumbersome bureaucracy which helped maintain the pyramid of his power had been a legacy dating back at least to the days of Muhammad Ali. Although, throughout his life, he was unwilling to share his supreme power, he himself failed to exercise it to any notable effect. When he died in 1970 Egypt had not been transformed to any degree commensurate with his early ambitions. He had made no formal dispositions for his succession, but the Vice-President was Anwar el-Sadat, and in 1970 it was he who succeeded, unopposed, to the presidency.

Anwar Sadat was an unknown quantity when he came to

power. He had not, like Abdul Hakim Amer or Ali Sabri, been part of Nasser's coterie of advisers in the Army, the police or the intelligence service, and as soon as he became President he found himself in conflict with them. Initially Sabri and other Nasserites thought Sadat would be an ideal front man for them to operate behind, just as General Neguib had been in 1952. However, Sadat soon showed that he was no easy prey. Between September 1970, when Nasser died, and May 1971, Sadat consolidated his position patiently. At every step his authority was challenged by Sabri and his ASU colleagues. Nine months after coming to power Sadat made lightning arrests of the ring-leaders and silenced his opponents by locking them up. Because he was recognised as Nasser's legitimate heir by the bulk of the population, and because he was, at the same time, untainted by the machinations of Nasserite power-politics, he was able to get away with this. Even the Army pledged their allegiance to him, in return for the promise of a prestigious role in post-Nasserite Egypt. The arrest of Sabri and his followers marked the final consolidation of Sadat's power.

Sadat inherited all the problems of Nasser's final years: an over-regulated economy which made it difficult to attract Western capital; the extensive influence of the Soviet Union as principal supplier of arms and military equipment; corresponding difficulties in relations with the United States; and, of course, the fact that, despite all Nasser's efforts since 1967, the Israeli Army was still in the Sinai Desert on the east bank of the Suez Canal and evinced no willingness to compromise with Egypt from its position of strength. Sadat had obviously learned a lot from observing Nasser in power. His advantage was that he could make concessions, as a newcomer, without giving the appearance of weakness. He embarked on a policy of political and economic liberalisation. He restricted the powers of the police and allowed more public discussion and criticism of the régime, especially in the press. And together with this came a new economic

160

liberalisation which he called 'infitah', an opening up, which will be described in the chapter on the economy.

He drafted a new constitution and had it approved by referendum in September 1971. A new National Assembly was set up which really did begin to debate and criticise government policy. Admittedly all members belonged to the sole permitted party, the ASU, duly purged of its Nasserite leadership and now unanimously loyal to Sadat. Nevertheless the changes were not purely cosmetic. They were, however, for the time being, secondary to the build-up of the armed forces which Sadat was concentrating on in preparation for administering the great shock to Israel which would, in the long run, drag her to the negotiating table.

The October War was a qualified military victory for Egypt but an important political victory for Sadat. He was hailed as the 'hero of the crossing' (of the Suez Canal) and the war made him a national leader and an international figure. He won the respect of many doubting Egyptians who had begun to feel that affairs had begun to drift since Nasser's death. After the war, with his hand immeasurably strengthened, he drew up a renewed programme for the expansion and development of the country, which he appropriately called the October Paper. Although it made no specific promises it emphasised the fact that Egyptian society would become stronger if it were opened up (infitah, again) and allowed to flower in greater freedom. The ASU was encouraged to extend its membership to grass-roots level, and by 1975 it had a membership of over four million and constituted a genuine sounding-board. With this expansion and pluralisation of the ASU, a groundswell of popular opinion made itself felt in favour of genuinely pluralistic political parties which would reflect the broad divisions of opinion within the ASU. It must be understood that real power still lay with Sadat and Sadat alone; the role of the political parties was not to form governments or assume any of the executive powers which were the prerogative of the President, but

161

they were to be simply a forum for debate. Nevertheless, the ASU served a useful purpose and gave the outside world an impression of democracy in action, albeit imperfectly.

By 1976 the ASU had split into three sections, one on the left, one on the right, and one mainstream centre party. The left-wing party was called the National Progressive Union Organisation (NPUO). It was led by the ex-Free Officer Khalid Muheiddin, and it advocated increased nationalisation of industry and more safeguards for workers. On the right was the Socialist Liberal Organisation (SLO) which supported capitalist free enterprise. In the centre stood the Arab Socialist Organisation (ASO) which supported Sadat's cautious middle-of-the-road liberalisation. In the general election of that year Sadat's ASO won a resounding victory in the National Assembly leaving the SLO and the NPUO on the margin with only 16 seats between them out of 350. After the election these factions of the ASU were renamed the National Progressive Union party, the Arab Socialist party and the Free Socialist party. The peripheral parties became extremely vocal in exercising their newly acquired right to criticise the Government and Sadat's leadership. In January 1977 there were sharp rises in the formerly heavily subsidised prices of some essential goods, and this provoked widespread rioting. Sadat had to call in the Army to restore order. He then – with some possible justification – blamed the extremist parties, especially the NPUP, for inciting the violence, and began to clamp down on the products of his liberalisation programme. He was not the first well-intentioned leader to find that a constitutional opposition is a difficult plant to propagate. Even with goodwill on both sides it is still a risky business of trial and error.

Sadat's solution, when the going got rough, was more sophisticated than Nasser's. After his own cathartic war with Israel in 1973 he showed greater imagination and possibly greater political courage than his predecessor. When he flew to Jerusalem in November 1977 he caused a political furore.

However, since the visit took everyone by surprise the opposition did not have a chance to muster much protest at the time. Only afterwards, and in response to the protracted Camp David negotiations, did protest grow until ultimately it was indirectly responsible for his assassination in 1981. (Camp David is covered in a later chapter.)

In July 1978 Sadat decided to form his own party, the National Democratic party, to replace the Arab Socialist party which already supported him. The object was to rein in the National Assembly. He also formed a new left-wing party called the Socialist Labour party, which was led by his brother-in-law. This time the object was to attract support away from the troublesome NPUP. After the signing of the peace treaty with Israel in 1979 new elections were held and, unsurprisingly, Sadat's NDP won an overwhelming majority while the NPUP won no seats at all. The SLP gained a modest 30 seats.

It is perhaps presumptuous of Western Europeans to pass hasty judgement on the imperfect working of liberal parliamentary democracy in emergent countries whose social and political foundations are alien to and unprepared for such a system. Even in those countries where it is an indigenous growth, parliamentary democracy and the multi-party system is an imperfect organism. So it may be unfair to criticise Sadat for experimenting with liberal policies such as the formation of opposition parties, and then clamping down on them as soon as they started to fulfil their function of scrutiny and criticism. In the homely metaphor of his own village origins, Sadat liked to see himself, and project the image of himself, as a benevolent father looking after his children, the Egyptian people, who needed to be kept in check for their own good. It was a less vainglorious self-image than Nasser's.

Of course, Sadat was adulated in the Western press for his role in the peacemaking with Israel, and he was aware of this. It flattered his ego. But at home he remained an

163

aloof figure. He wielded as much power as Nasser, but with less obvious relish. He did not want to be a dictator. He would, no doubt, have liked to fulfil the role of a moderate, democratic head of state, if only Egypt had already been a country with moderate, democratic political traditions. But the ordinary people did not feel constrained to love him for expecting too much of them. The fact that he was a man of culture who liked to consort with diplomats and intellectuals, set a distance between him and the ordinary people. Nasser, the autocrat, was loved and respected by the people, while Sadat, the would-be liberal, left them cold.

When, on 6 October 1981, Sadat was assassinated by Muslim extremists at a military parade in Cairo, his death did not bring weeping crowds out on the streets as Nasser's death had done in 1970. The public response at home was one of stunned, wary silence. Outside Egypt there was a sense of loss comparable with, though not equal to, that felt at the death of John F. Kennedy. Rare, after all, are those statesmen who even once step outside their customary reactive role and actually take a positive step to change the course of historical events.

Israel and the United States were concerned on two counts: first they were worried that his successor might abrogate the peace treaty with Israel, and secondly they were afraid that even if Mubarak remained committed to the treaty, he might soon in turn be assassinated or otherwise disposed of, like the Shah, by an Islamic fundamentalist rising. Both these fears were well founded, but neither was born out by events. Sadat's successor proved quite capable of taking matters in hand efficiently and, where necessary, ruthlessly. On the other side of the fence, Arab states hostile to the Egyptian–Israel treaty were jubiliant. In Damascus there was dancing in the streets at the news of Sadat's murder. The Syrian leader, Hafez al-Assad, must have had an uncomfortable feeling that many more Syrians would have taken to the streets if he himself had been the victim.

Immediately after the assassination, Vice-President Hosni Mubarak, who was actually on the reviewing stand at the moment Sadat was killed, declared a national state of emergency to last for one year. A week later he was elected President of the Republic by referendum. At the time of the killing the armed forces pledged themselves to 'safeguard the integrity and stability of the nation at all cost . . . and to repel all threats to the freedom and dignity of Egypt'. Only a few days later this was put to the test when Mubarak ordered the Army into Assiyut, a major city of Upper Egypt and a traditional hotbed of Islamic fundamentalist agitation. The uprising there continued for several weeks but was finally put down firmly and successfully.

Hosni Mubarak had been looked upon as something of a dark horse under Sadat, and this gave rise to some apprehensions. As it turned out those fears were totally unjustified. Mubarak soon demonstrated that he had his own mature style of government, quite different from Sadat's style of public presidential rule. Mubarak had risen to power in the aftermath of the October War in 1973, when he had distinguished himself as head of the Airforce. In 1975 Sadat promoted him to the vice-presidency, and there is no doubt that he was being groomed for supreme power as the first of a new rising generation. With unquestioned and possibly unquestioning loyalty, Mubarak was, for six years, Sadat's right-hand man. He often represented him on trips abroad. He earned a reputation for being adept at 'palace' intrigue.

As President he enjoys strong support from the armed forces, especially the Airforce. His style of government is low-key compared with that of either Nasser or Sadat, and unlike Sadat he keeps his private life private. He will not allow his work to intrude into his personal affairs. He has emerged as a strong, resolute and solid leader in whom Egypt can place great hopes. He has travelled widely since becoming President, and raised a discreet and always moderating voice on issues affecting the Middle East. Because he has not sought to create dramatic military or diplomatic diversions, domestic criticism has occasionally been voiced at his alleged failure to do more to tackle the country's dire economic problems. It may well be that some of his critics preferred the extravagant panaceas of Sadat's 'infitah'; some of them no doubt belong to the small new capitalist class which fed on the wave of Western investment in the 1970s and whose tactless conspicuous consumption did so much to encourage the rise of ascetic Islamic fundamentalist fervour. It may yet be shown that Mubarak's more measured approach is more likely to bring about the long-term social reforms and economic development on which the future standard of living of the people will depend.

There is no doubt that the main problem confronting Mubarak is the force of Islamic fundamentalism. He also has to fear the wrath of radical Arab states opposed to the peace treaty with Israel. The assassin's gun could easily be aimed at him from either quarter, and could throw Egypt once again into turmoil.

3

The Army

This chapter will look at the Army as a modern Egyptian institution. It will describe the growth of the Army, from being an insignificant social group on the fringe of society at the beginning of the twentieth century, to becoming a strong, cohesive social force. By 1952 it was able successfully to challenge the democratic parliamentary system and assume total control of the country with scarcely a shot fired. Then we shall see how, from 1952 to 1056, the small nucleus of 'Free Officers' who inspired and led the revolution consolidated their power and made a return to representative government impossible. It was during these four years that the unofficial leader of the group, Gamal Nasser, emerged as the unchallenged leader of Egypt.

When, on the morning of 23 July 1952, Anwar Sadat announced on Cairo Radio that the 'Free Officers' coup had taken place 'on behalf of Egypt', the reaction of most Egyptians was one of relief that the social upheaval and near chaos of the previous six months was over. At that moment people from nearly all sections of society saw the Army as the antidote to mob rule. The recent history of Lebanon illustrates how appalling that situation can be, and we have seen how Egypt had already had to be rescued once in the nineteenth century from such a fate by foreign intervention. In 1952 the Egyptian Army, weak as it was relative to external enemies, was the most stable and politically cohesive unit in the country. It was also technologically more advanced than other groups because it alone had been the recipient of foreign aid and weapons since the Second World War. The key political motive for the 1952 coup was 'national regeneration'. Even today this is considered an acceptable reason for making a bid for power against an established régime. In 1952 the Army proudly called itself the 'saviour of the nation' and it was from this claim that they derived their legitimacy.

In order to understand the behaviour of the military élite that emerged in 1952 we must look briefly into the origins of the Egyptian Army. The military establishment dates back to Muhammad Ali, that benevolent Albanian autocrat who managed to concentrate both political and economic power in his own hands at the expense of competing princes after the expulsion of Napoleon from Egypt. Until the Napoleonic conquest, internal security had been assured by a system of military feudalism under which mercenary troops served the ruling prince or 'bey' in return for a fiefdom off which they could live. There was, consequently, no idea of a national army, since the mercenaries, called 'spahis', were non-Egyptians. The fiefdoms they received as a token of gratitude from the Ottoman Sultan or his representative were often hereditary, and the system produced a mercenary, foreign caste of soldiers. Native Egyptians were not allowed to develop a military tradition. There was no military conscription and, until Muhammad Ali, Egyptians were only enlisted into the ranks; the officers were always Albanian, Circassian, Turkish, and the like. Since Muhammad Ali considered a strong army essential to the building of a modern state, in 1820 he set up a Military College in Aswan under the direction of a Frenchman, Colonel Sèvres, and there the first 500 Egyptian officers received their training. By 1830 this and other colleges had produced a whole new cadre. Yet, far from creating a new vanguard of Egyptian soldiers who would encourage their countrymen from all walks of life to take part in the national development, the newly trained Egyptians became almost alienated foreigners in their own land, imitating their foreign instructors and divorcing themselves from Egyptian society as a whole. Muhammad Ali took care that this emergent military group never assumed any political power in the country – their efforts were directed towards colonisation of the Sudan. He merely added this new military cadre to those other aspects of national life concentrated under his personal control.

When Ali's successor, Said Pasha, introduced a one-year conscription law, this did indeed produce the nucleus of a standing army of native Egyptians, controlled by low-ranking Egyptians officers and high-ranking foreign officers. Ismail, the 'great Europeaniser', paid great attention to the training and education of Egyptians along European lines, and it was he who established the military college at Abbasiya, near Cairo, which is to this day the major centre for military instruction. Under Ismail a publicity campaign was launched extolling the benefits of joining the Egyptian Army, and all this served to give the native officer corps a sense of identity and professional pride. Just as Ismail's Consultative Assembly gave the emerging native bourgeoisie a political voice in national affairs, so now this same class was given access to power, and it quickly came into conflict with the ruling dynasty.

From the military standpoint, disaffection with the Khedive stemmed from his acquiescence in the system of Dual Control of the country's finances by Britain and France. Some Egyptian historians have claimed that the Orabist revolt was a 'nationalist' uprising, but Egyptian nationalism was not a real force until the beginning of the twentieth century. Zaglul and the Wafd were truly Egyptian nationalists, but Orabi was simply a junior officer in the Army, of native stock, who, without being politically sophisticated, embodied the national spirit of the age. Orabi Pasha had the ability to inflame the Egyptian people to take to the streets

169

and protest at European domination of their affairs, and also at the fact that the leadership of their country was totally controlled by non-native Egyptians, who owned vast tracts of land and exploited their fellow countrymen. And he belonged to the only section of native Egyptian society that the people felt was capable of influencing events: the nascent Army.

In 1882 the Army learned an important political lesson: namely, that it could decisively affect political events in the country by using brute force. In the case of Orabi, of course, he was released from trial by court martial through the intervention of his military comrades who arrested the military judges trying him. When he was eventually appointed Minister for War, another lesson was learned: that the Army, through military threats, could affect political appointments. This was a grave precedent. In 1882 only British intervention had propped up the Khedive and his régime. When a similar situation occurred in 1952 there was no foreign power prepared to intervene and assume the political and military responsibility Britain had undertaken seventy years before.

It is important to look at the British occupation of Egypt from 1882 to 1952 in proper historical perspective. In the light of the 1980s it seems barely conceivable that Britain should have expended so much man-power and resources on an area of the world so remote from the great majority of her people. A century ago Britain's sense of global responsibility was much greater than today, but of course she also expected compensatory economic and strategic rights. Under the British occupation the Egyptian Army was totally subservient to the British GOC. While the British needed native Egyptian man-power in the ranks of a new Middle Eastern Force, they felt unable to grant any political freedom to an officer class that might one day, they felt, take the initiative that its predecessors had done in 1882. They consequently gave a minimum amount of training to new recruits.

During the First World War, Egypt became an armed camp for the British, Australian and other Commonwealth soldiers. The war-time economy boomed as a result of high demand and the foreign currency pouring into the country. When, in 1914, the British officially declared Egypt a Protectorate, Egyptians saw this as a positive gesture designed to encourage them to help the war effort, but also as a prelude to post-war independence and sovereignty. When, at the end of the war, they realised it had been a mere expedient to secure their temporary acquiescence, their anger exploded in mass protests against the British. When they saw Britain and France claiming the spoils of victory and dividing up the Middle East into spheres of influence, they became aware that the British had no intention of relinquishing their hold on Egypt and were even looking for fresh ways to prolong the legitimacy of their rule in the area. They watched Britain and France operating their respective Mandates over Palestine and Syria, ostensibly to prepare those countries for independence, and they came to the conclusion this was simply an ingenious system designed to dominate without the stigma attached to open colonisation or annexation.

In 1922 Britain unilaterally declared Egypt independent. But she still retained several important cards: her right to defend imperial communications, which included the Suez Canal and could even cover renewed military occupation if she considered it necessary; and the retention of a British Inspector General of the Egyptian Armed Forces. Thus, in effect, right up to 1936 the Army was Egyptian-manned but British-commanded. But in that year a new Anglo-Egyptian treaty wrought a change of incalculable significance. The doors of the Military College were thrown open to Egyptians from nearly all levels of society. Hitherto, financial and other restrictive qualifications had limited intake to a relatively privileged few. Now, too, there was to be an Egyptian Inspector of the Armed Forces. A not inconsiderable quid pro quo was that all arms were to be purchased from Britain. The first year's intake of trainees contained several names that were to be heard again, including Gamal Nasser, Anwar Sadat and Abdul Hakim Amer. Links forged between members of that small group were to play a crucial part in building up that spirit of organisational efficiency combined with secrecy which was to characterise the 'Free Officers' and their supporters after the Second World War.

The new post-1936 class of Egyptian officers were not interested in the existing political parties. They felt the Wafd had burnt itself out, and they cast around for other ideologies. The old parliamentary system appeared weak and uninspiring to these young soldiers who felt that the new, strong Egypt that was emerging should have a new Egyptian ideology to give the nation a national sense of direction. All had been active in anti-British agitation over withdrawal from the Canal Zone and British support for Jewish settlement in Palestine. The rising power of Nazi Germany and Fascist Italy, with their glorification of military and paramilitary cadres, all focused attention on the possibilities for political action outside the ambit of the Wafd or the other small parliamentary parties. Moreover, now that Britain was committed to negotiating over the Canal issue, the Wafd had lost one of the main planks of its popular programme, and it seemed to have lost impetus. So during the period from 1936 to 1949 the new class of officers developed their political philosophy. All were concerned about the future of their country and disillusioned with their autocratic King, whose interests, they felt, did not coincide with those of Egypt as a whole. Steadily they gained in maturity and political sophistication. During the Second World War, Egyptian troops did not take part in the fighting, but they provided services and support for British and Commonwealth troops stationed in Egypt. Incidents like the notorious February 4th Affair, when the British ambassador forced King Farouk to appoint Nahas Pasha, the Wafd leader, as Prime Minister and intimidated the King with a British military force surrounding the royal palace, made a resounding impact on Egyptian public attitudes. However pressing the justification for the incident, it deeply offended many Egyptians, and Nasser often recalled it later in his anti-British harangues.

As early as 1948 the new Egyptian Army had a chance to see action for the first time, when the provisional Jewish Government in Tel Aviv declared the independence of the state of Israel and Egypt joined other Arab nations in attacking the new state. The end of the Palestine War had not been a foregone conclusion and Israeli troops fought off invading forces at odds of up to seventy to one. After the Armistice Egyptian troops withdrew to the Sinai and the small Gaza strip. The defeat was not calamitous but it was felt as a great humiliation for the new Army. It produced fierce recriminations within the Army and rumours of callous incompetence in the General Staff, and profiteering by the King and the Government in Cairo through supplying faulty equipment and failing to make supplies available where they were most needed. For the small group of officers who had known each other since their years together at the Military Academy in 1936, the Palestine War was a turning point. Throughout the 1940s they had maintained a loosely-bound friendship which could not be called an organisation. It had no ideological cohesion. Sadat, for example, had tried to defect to the incoming Axis forces in the Western desert and had made contacts with the Muslim Brotherhood; Nasser and his good friend Abdul Hakim Amer served in the Sudan together and shared a contempt for both the palace and the British. But until the Palestine War the Army saw no practical role for itself other than that of maintaining public order.

The humiliating defeat in Palestine produced two reactions in the Army: first, it showed how much needed to be done within the Army if it was to become an efficient fighting force; and secondly, it aroused a deep sense of betrayal at the hands of the King. This disaffection for the King led to distrust of the whole constitutional system and encouraged sympathy between the Army and radical groups opposed both to the King and the constitution. There was the feeling that, just as an occupying power had to be expelled from the land, so, too, should these inadequate government institutions be banished.

In 1949 the Free Officers, as the secret group called itself, met and elected an Executive Council with Nasser as its chairman. This is the first time we hear of the Free Officers and there is no record of the actual date of its formation. By 1949, however, the Free Officers were using their positions in the Military Academy and the Staff College to recruit new members and infiltrate sensitive military posts. They began to publish pamphlets and set up a secret cell-system. By 1951 an intense struggle was in progress between an increasingly suspicious King and an increasingly suspicious Army. The Army capitalised on the massive discontent and unrest in the country and on its own position as the only stable force capable of bringing about change. Nevertheless, in the months prior to their planned coup there was always a danger that they might be pre-empted by royalist officers and troops. The coup, on 23 July 1952, succeeded because the Free Officers and their supporters had correctly identified the spirit of popular discontent and because they were closer, in social and economic terms, to the bulk of Army officers than they were to those high-ranking officers who remained loyal to the King.

Once the successful coup was achieved, the Free Officers proceeded to establish control over the country and consolidate their grip on all aspects of national life. In the months immediately after the coup the Revolutionary Command Council, as the Free Officers styled themselves in government, left the door open for civilian participation and even a return to parliamentary democracy. But they insisted that the old political parties 'purge' themselves of undesirable elements and reform their internal organisation. The truth was that the RCC, having assumed power, did not know where to go. It had no real policies of its own, and for the first year, until 1953, its main concern was to maintain order and try to earn some claim to legitimacy in the eyes of the people. The most obvious means to this end was to promise an early return to parliamentary democracy, but without King Farouk. The Army dared not make an overt bid for total political power until the complete loyalty of all sections of the military command had been ascertained, thus guaranteeing the safety of the RCC and reassuring the outside world that it was there to stay. So although King Farouk had been exiled, his son was named Regent and a republic was not declared until 1953. Then the RCC set about building their alternative. The old political parties were dissolved and a new mass organisation was launched called the Liberation Rally, which was intended to fill the gap between the RCC and the people. They also set up an ineffectual body called the Islamic Congress as a sop to Islamic opinion and a bid to broaden their image. Nasser consolidated his position as undisputed leader of the RCC and set about silencing any vocal criticsm among students and journalists. Step by step the Army became institutionalised as the new, legitimate Government. One event in particular cemented Nasser's position as supreme leader of the country. On 26 October 1954, while he was addressing a large crowd in Alexandria, an attempt was made on his life by a member of the Muslim Brotherhood. It was unsuccessful, but that day he became a self-declared martyr: 'If I die you are all Gamal Abdel Nassers,' he shouted. From that moment his star was in the ascendant and he was effectively unstoppable.

By 1955 he had become an international figure on the world stage, ranking with Nehru and Tito as a leader of a non-aligned nation. In those first three years the group of Free Officers had transformed itself from a conspiratorial band of soldiers, who had been shrewd enough to take advantage of national discontent, into a new ruling élite with power of patronage and censure extending, at will, to cover any individual and any section of society. It had done this by dissociating itself from the earlier civilian 'nationalist' movements and creating new political expressions of this popular feeling. The Liberation Rally was later replaced by the broader-based Arab Socialist Union. While some attempt had to be made to give the régime an Islamic flavour, this was done chiefly by emphasising anti-European themes, and support was carefully withheld from the extremist Muslim Brotherhood, which constituted a political threat. In addition, economic policies, designed to promote greater social equality, were sure to find favour with the underprivileged mass of the population.

During 1955, the Soviet Union, now recovering economically from the near-defeat of the Second World War, began to make overtures to Egypt and capitalise on the strained relations at that time between Egypt and the West. Nasser had refused to be drawn into any of the Western-inspired post-war security pacts aimed against the Soviet Union, especially the Baghdad Pact creating a northern tier of states to protect the Middle East from Soviet encroachment, and as a result of his attitude the West had ceased to send him arms. So he turned the tables in the only way he could; he asked the new Soviet bloc for arms. In 1955 an arms deal was concluded between Egypt and Czechoslovakia, and this was read as a signal of the beginning of Soviet military commitment in the area. It brought the cold war to the Middle East.

The Czech arms deal was important for Egypt in that it opened the door to an alternative source of arms and reduced the influence of the West over Egypt. When, shortly after the arms deal, America withdrew its offer to finance the High Dam project at Aswan, far from pressurising Egypt to toe a more Western line, it threw her even further into the arms of the Soviet Union. By the middle of 1956 Egypt had acquired Russian-made planes, tanks and rockets. The abrupt withdrawal of American aid for the High Dam project was the one action which, more than anything else, made Nasser decide to 'punish' the West and nationalise the Suez Canal.

On 26 July 1956, in a speech at Alexandria commemorating the fourth anniversary of Farouk's exile, and standing in the same square where the attempt had earlier been made on his life, Nasser declared that Egypt was nationalising the Suez Canal and that Egyptian troops were moving in to occupy the Canal Zone. He was wreaking a bitter revenge for 4 February 1942. 'Lord Killearn,' he thundered, 'we all know Lord Killearn. [He had formerly been Sir Miles Lampson.] 'He stood up in the British House of Lords and insulted Egypt . . . I met the British ambassador at my house and told him . . . we could not take such an insult. . . uttered by MPs and lords. . . and in particular by Lord Killearn.'

The reaction throughout the Arab World was one of delight, and the act of nationalisation raised Nasser to the status of the international Arab spokesman and leader. The history of the Suez War is well known. Briefly, Britain and France persuaded Israel that she should strike back at Egyptian commandos who had been infiltrating into Israeli territory from the Gaza Strip, and should advance towards the Suez Canal. Britain and France would then demand a cease-fire and require both Egyptian and Israeli forces to withdraw from the Canal Zone. They would then move in themselves to fill the gap and regain control of the Canal. And that is just what happened. The only credible motive for the whole devious procedure would have been a desire to avoid offending the Arab World through an act of unvarnished aggression. But proof of collusion was evident from the fact that Britain and France issued their ultimatum for withdrawal before the Israelis even reached the Canal. Nasser was hardly likely to foresee that Anthony Eden, the British Prime Minister, would be so reckless as to actually attack Egypt in concert wth Israel, and thereby allow himself to be branded not only as an aggressor but an aggressor in league with Israel, the arch-enemy of the Arabs. In the event there was not much the Egyptian Army could do to stop the Anglo-French advance, even though it fought courageously. It was saved by the United Nations which expressed universal condemnation of the aggression and called for an immediate and unconditional withdrawal of all forces from Egypt. Both the Soviet Union and the United States insisted that Britain and France halt hostilities. British prestige and credibility were at their lowest ebb, as was the value of sterling. It was these factors, rather than Egyptian military prowess, that ensured the survival of Nasser's régime in 1956. Quantities of Egyptian equipment were captured or destroyed, but this was soon replaced by the Soviet Union, who further strengthened her position of influence in Egypt. The dangerous result of the Suez War was that, while Britain and France had withdrawn because of international pressure, Nasser was able to lead the Egyptian people into believing this had been brought about by the strength of the Egyptian Army. This induced a completely false sense of confidence in the Army, and eventually he seemed to have convinced himself, too. This unwarranted faith in the Army was not to be put to the test until the next war with Israel, ten years later.

Meanwhile, Egypt kept the Suez Canal closed to Israeli shipping and goaded Israel into taking action about it. In 1959, for example, Nasser was saying: 'If Ben Gurion or Moshe Dayan is looking for the final battle, I am announcing in the name of the people, the people of the United Arab Republic, that we are waiting for that final battle in order to rid ourselves of the Israeli abomination.' And Israel, for her part, announced her acceptance of the Eisenhower doctrine so that she would qualify for American arms to

178

counter the mounting Russian-supplied arsenal in Egypt. By 1962 both Egypt and Israel had acquired rockets and a regional arms race was well under way.

Egypt's union with Syria from 1958 to 1961 was a further political move in the line-up against Israel. After a series of military coups in 1949–51 the parliamentary system bequeathed to Syria by the French had been abandoned. In 1958 the Ba'ath party had assumed power with a Nasser-like régime, and at the same time the opposition had taken a lurch to the left. Lacking a reliable army of its own, the Ba'athist government was constrained to accept Egyptian help to control the domestic situation. While the United Arab Republic lasted the Egyptian Army served as an extension of the Syrian security forces. A corollary to this was, not unnaturally, that Syrian national interests tended for this period to be subordinated to those of Egypt. The Syrian Army was dominated by imported Egyptian officers. One Syrian General complained: 'Every Egyptian officer during the union acted as if he were Gamal Abdul Nasser in person, and Syrian officers felt demoralised. . .' Eventually, on 28 September 1961, Syrian Army units stationed around Damascus simply marched on the city and proclaimed the end of the United Arab Republic. It could be argued that this action in itself demonstrated that they had learned something from their mentors and become a more determined, positive force than they had been when they submitted to the Egyptian presence three years before. Secession from the UAR was a military decision, not a political one.

The break-up of the United Arab Republic was a severe set-back for Nasser's prestige and also for the Army, which had not been able to prevent the split. Within a few weeks, and possibly as a means of distracting public attention, Nasser committed Egyptian troops to the republican side in the Yemen Civil War. It was their first taste of action outside Egypt. The new Imam of North Yemen (South Yemen was called Aden at this time and was a British colony) had been forced by republican troops to flee his capital. He was supported by traditionalist Saudi Arabia, and a proxy war was then waged between Egypt and Saudi Arabia, which dragged on until 1965, by which time some 70,000 Egyptian troops were engaged in a pointless war that did not directly benefit Egypt.

In 1964 the Arab League announced the formation of a unified military command to co-ordinate action against Israel. The League, it will be remembered, had been devised by the British as a means of channelling Pan-Arab sentiments into line with British interests, but Nasser had usurped it, and its headquarters in Cairo had come to symbolise the heart of the Arab World. Whether Nasser really intended to attack Israel, or whether his threats were just rhetoric designed to impress other Arab states and his fellow countrymen, is a debatable question. What must have been clear to both Israelis and Egyptians, however, was that only by launching a pre-emptive strike into the Israeli heartland did Egypt stand a chance of catching Israel off guard. Presumably Nasser must have been fairly confident of the Army's capabilities, for on 16 May 1967 he ordered the United Nations Emergency Force out of their observation posts on the Straits of Tiran, through which all Israeli shipping must pass on its way to the southern port of Eilat, and on 23 May Egyptian troops closed the Straits. Nasser must have expected the Israelis to react to such a blow to their only south-bound shipping-lane. On 30 May King Hussein of Jordan arrived in Cairo and signed a defence agreement with Nasser. A concerted propaganda campaign from Amman, Damascus, Cairo and Baghdad gave vent to all the pent-up sense of humiliation felt by the Arab World with regard to Israel ever since its creation in 1948. The deteriorating situation gave the Israeli Government little choice but to take action against what it perceived as a threat to its very existence. On 5 June the Israeli Airforce bombed Egyptian airfields, destroying over 300 of the 400 fighter

180

aircraft awaiting Nasser's order to take off in attack against Israel. That same day crack Israeli troops advanced deep into Sinai towards the Suez Canal, as they had done eleven years before, and by 8 June they had reached the Canal. The shock for Nasser was so great that for some time he could not believe it. The Egyptian Army, the pride and symbol of national independence and strength, had been utterly routed in less than four days. Nasser first accused the Americans of actively fighting with Israel. Then he turned on his lifelong friend from Military Academy days, Abdel Hakim Amer, who had been in command of the Egyptian forces as they tried to retreat across the Canal. Amer later committed suicide. And if the Egyptians suffered a psychological blow, so also did the Soviet Union, who had supplied nearly all their equipment. Soviet credibility as defender of the Arabs against Israel and the United States was seriously impaired.

Why were the Egyptians so easily defeated at the hands of a much smaller army fighting on three fronts with a fraction of the population of Egypt, let alone of Egypt allied with Syria and Jordan? The answer can only lie in the social composition of the competing armies. Essentially, Israel was a Western-orientated country with a comparatively strong military and industrial infrastructure and a population totally committed to fighting for the defence of their country. They really felt that if the land they and their parents and grandparents had striven so hard to develop were to be over-run by the Arabs, it would be destroyed for good together with their new Israeli society. Egypt, by contrast, was a large country with a large population struggling for subsistence and grappling with appalling economic and social problems as its traditional Islamic society emerged in confrontation with the West and its new values. Egyptian soldiers, usually badly educated and from varied and mainly poor social backgrounds, could not often identify with their commanding officers, who seemed aloof and out of touch with their troops.

Immediately after the defeat of 1967 Nasser resigned; but

181

this was probably no more than a tactical move to bring the nation out on the streets to call him back. Egypt *was* Nasser, and the man in the street saw no real alternative – even had he been inclined to look for one – but to ask him to stay. There was, in any case, no formula for electing a new leader or even finding a temporary substitute, since all the political institutions, like the Arab Socialist Union, were mere organs for maintaining Nasser in power. As one leading writer put it at the time: 'No wonder we clung to our leader after the defeat, and that we made his personal existence a substitute for victory, or a synonym for it, because he had made us feel in every possible way that there existed in Egypt and the whole Arab World only one intelligence, one power, one personality.' So, after massive popular demonstrations in his support, Nasser withdrew his resignation and set about re-establishing his authority. However, after his set-back, the people were not prepared to accept him as uncritically as they had done before 1967, and there was increasing disaffection among students and workers.

At the same time, clashes were multiplying across the Suez Canal between Egyptians and Israelis. Egypt sank the Israeli destroyer *Eilat*, and Israel retaliated by bombing oil-refineries at Suez. These clashes grew more serious and on several occasions almost erupted into open hostilities. This period became known as the 'War of Attrition'. Commando raids and deep-penetration air-strikes were regular occurrences. The Soviet Union had by now replaced much of the equipment destroyed in the 1967 War and began to use her own troops to patrol the Canal Zone. By August 1970 the futility of this sporadic fighting persuaded both sides to agree to a cease-fire.

In September 1970 Nasser died. Suddenly a whole era came to an end. There was no obvious replacement for the leader who had dominated Egyptian national life for eighteen years. A power struggle ensued among his followers and his critics. Accession to supreme power is never smooth, nor without risk, especially for a national leader who has risen in the shadow of so autocratic and authoritarian a man as Nasser.

Anwar Sadat had been appointed Vice-President by Nasser nine months before his death. At the time he was virtually unknown in the country at large. In 1936 he had been one of the Free Officers and been one of Nasser's close band of associates at the Military Academy. Before and during the Second World War he had close links with the Muslim Brotherhood, and in 1941 he had hoped for an Axis victory as a means of eliminating British influence from Egypt. He had been Secretary of the Islamic Congress when it was set up in 1952, and later Secretary of the National Union, and Speaker of the National Assembly – all of which were ineffectual institutions designed to lend legitimacy to Nasser's rule without impairing his freedom of action. Such a series of sinecures did not pave the way to his unchallenged promotion to Vice-President, let alone to his assumption of the Nasser heritage in 1070. A group of Nasser's supporters, under the leadership of Ali Sabri, another of the Free Officers, saw themselves as more legitimate heirs. Their origins were more aristocratic, unlike the majority of his colleagues, and they were happy to see Sadat in place as a figurehead only until their moment came to make a counter-bid for power. Sadat forced a showdown with Sabri. He named his own charges against them, and in 1971 Sabri and 91 of his supporters were sentenced to long terms of imprisonment.

Having eliminated serious competition for power, Sadat turned to deal with the two main legacies of the Nasser era: first, the close ties with the Soviet Union, and consequent ostracism by the West, and notably by the United States; and secondly, the Israeli occupation of Egyptian territory in the Sinai Desert which Nasser had not been able to challenge effectively. It was not easy to free himself from the grip of the Soviet Union, which had a monopoly on arms

183

supplies to Egypt, but through liberalising political and economic measures he distanced himself from Soviet leaders and began to endear himself to Washington. His intentions regarding Israel and the Sinai took rather longer to mature. Since Egypt's social problems were not susceptible to short-term solution, he needed a military success. The Army remained solidly behind him, and he and a few very senior Army commanders came to two conclusions: first, they reasoned that all the while they relied on the Soviet Union for arms, the United States would ensure that Israel kept ahead in the regional arms race; moreover, only America could force Israel to make concessions. Secondly, they calculated that the territorial stalemate in the region would only be broken if a severe shock could be administered to the Israeli High Command to jolt it out of the complacency it had been basking in since its 1967 victory. So Sadat began to make peaceful approaches to the United States on the one hand and to Israel on the other, while at the same time continuing to accept deliveries of Soviet arms. The planning had begun for a surprise war that was to change the power balance in the region for ever. By July 1972, having absorbed large amounts of Soviet military hardware, he felt it expedient to prove his good intentions to the West by expelling about 15,000 Soviet military advisers from Egypt, to the unconcealed delight of the United States and Israel. Whether or not this was a purely tactical move designed to lull Israel into a sense of false security, it certainly deeply offended the Russians, who never forgave him.

By the autumn of 1973, with a large arsenal of Soviet arms, an increasing measure of good will from Washington and dismissive contempt from Tel Aviv, Sadat was ready to administer his shock. On 6 October, Egyptian troops stormed the famous 'invincible' Bar-Lev line of fortifications that ran the length of the Israeli bank of the Suez Canal. Simultaneously, Syrian troops attacked lightly defended Israeli positions on the Golan Heights and advanced on to the Golan plateau. The Israelis were taken totally off their guard and it took them nearly two weeks to turn the tide and push back the two-pronged attack. Several observers commented afterwards that if Egypt had not stopped to re-group her forces after they had crossed the Canal in the first days of the war, Israel would have had to withdraw troops from the Golan front to the Sinai and her whole Army might have been over-stretched and even, ultimately, over-whelmed. As it was, Prime Minister Golda Meir successfully appealed to the United States to airlift arms to Israel, and at one point it was reported that American planes were flying directly from abroad to the combat zones without even landing in Israel to unload first. Although Israel eventually 'won' in the sense that she occupied more territory at the end of the war than before – Israeli troops were on the highway from Suez to Cairo and only fifteen miles from Damascus – she had in fact suffered a serious defeat. As Sadat said: 'The myth of (Israel's) invincible airforce, armoury and soldiers has been shattered at last.' Israel lost 2,552 dead or missing. Egypt lost some 9,000 men killed and another 11,000 were wounded. Yet despite the very high cost in lives and material, the war had served its purpose. Egypt now felt she could treat Israel as an equal, and Israel was obliged, at least temporarily, to revise her ideas of invincible military supremacy in the area. After 1973 peace with Israel would no longer be the equivalent to capitulation, as it would have seemed after the 1967 War.

The 1973 War established Sadat as a national figure – the 'hero of the crossing' – although he never attained anything like the mythical stature of Nasser. The Army had regained its honour, and finally come of age as a professional body of men whose job it was to defend Egypt from external threats, not just to be an extension of an internal police force to maintain a dictator in power. It had shed its role as a ruling élite and withdrawn to that role normally occupied by armies in Western democracies; namely that of a responsible, professional body of soldiers accepting orders from civilians. Army commanders and men alike submitted willingly to their new status and showed increasing reluctance to become involved in politics. There was a deep feeling among all ranks that Nasser, for all his adulation of the Army, had undermined it as a professional body by forcing it into such a key role in the every-day maintenance of the national power-structure, and that in times of emergency it had not always been capable of producing the response required to repel outside threats. The Army notably demonstrated its unwillingness to intervene in internal affairs in January 1977 at the time when rioters protested against the removal of subsidies on essential commodities. Sadat asked the Prime Minister, Mamduh Salem, to request that the Chief of Staff, Gamasy, send in troops to dispel the rioters. But the latter reminded Salem, and Sadat, of the promise made by Army leaders after the October War that never again would the Army be used against the civilian population. Gamasy declared that unless the cuts in subsidies were rescinded, he could not be responsible for the behaviour of his troops. Sadat acquiesced. This illustrates an important change in the attitude of Army leaders. Under Nasser, they would have been only too delighted to join in the fray in the hope of reward from their political master. Under Sadat, they gave responsible advice which was not presented as a challenge to Sadat's executive power, but rather as the proper and professional opinion of the armed forces. This should not be interpreted as marking a reduction in their power, but rather a change of emphasis. No Egyptian President under present circumstances could rule without at least the tacit support of the military.

Sadat's Vice-President, Hosni Mubarak, was Commander of the Egyptian Airforce at the time of the 1973 War. He furnished a useful channel for communication and liaison between the Army and the presidency. He deservedly enjoyed considerable personal popularity within the armed forces for the performance of the Airforce during the war. When Sadat made him Vice-President in 1975, he may have seen this as a means of fending off criticism over the protracted negotiations he was conducting to remove the Israelis from Sinai. Some Egyptian military leaders felt he could have achieved this by force in the early days of the war in Sinai had the political will existed to promote such an action. Mubarak's appointment did go some way towards reassuring them that they had one of their men near the centre of decision-making. Mubarak fulfilled his role as Vice-President obstensibly in a ceremonial capacity rather than as a competitive ex-soldier. He played the part of Sadat's loyal lieutenant, paying state visits abroad and sharing the burden of state functions. He cultivated extensive contacts with African leaders and their armed forces, while Sadat showed more direct interest in Asian affairs. During the Sadat–Mubarak period (1975–81) Egyptian policy developed an interesting Asian–African balance which Nasser had, unsuccessfully, attempted to bring about. Although Mubarak was undoubtedly powerful during Sadat's presidency, he was careful never to step out of line, and in fact he became quite noted for the glib and fatuous smile he wore at all state functions where Sadat was present. Egypt nicknamed him 'la vache qui rit' after the advertisements in Arabic broadcast by Radio Monte Carlo to the Arab World.

Mubarak was, then, an unknown quantity at the time of Sadat's assassination in 1981. He had always remained scrupulously loyal to the President, despite periodic rumours of conspiracy in the Army. In the wake of the assassination, both American and Israeli concern focused on the unknown and therefore unpredictable qualities of the new President.

The assassination carried no important military implications. The Speaker of the National Assembly became interim President, prior to the presidential elections, but real power immediately fell to Hosni Mubarak, and there has never been any question from those first moments of his total control of the military establishment.

Has there been any noticeable change in the style of the Egyptian military since Mubarak took office? It might be suggested that the Army leaders are less reticent about using military might to quash domestic revolt than they were in 1977. Certainly, when a revolt of adherents of the Islamic Fundamentalists who assassinated Sadat broke out in Assiyut soon after that event, Mubarak did not hesitate to demand and obtain the support of the military to suppress it ruthlessly and effectively. But that was, perhaps, a special case. The uprising at Assiyut might, if left unchecked, have toppled the whole political and military régime, Iranian style. The Iranian experience has taught the Egyptian leadership a great deal. Until the Iranian revolution in 1979, nobody quite believed that an autocratic, seemingly omnipotent ruler like the Shah could really be removed from power by a popular religious upheaval. By the same token the Iranian experience has shown popular mass movements like the Islamic Fundamentalists in other Arab countries, the extent of their potential strength. President Mubarak must work very hard to create a stable political middle ground in Egypt if he and the whole existing political structure are not to be swept away by the legacy of his predecessors.

4

Religion

The Islamic religion has been the most important factor regulating the social evolution of Egypt ever since it was brought into the country by Arab invaders under Ibn el-As, who swept along the North African coast from the Arabian peninsular in 641 AD. Before their arrival, Egypt had been a Christian country. Some of the earliest Greek Christians had settled there and set up governmental institutions, and there was a minority of Coptic Christians who had maintained their own language, Coptic, which was a late form of ancient Egyptian. The Arab invaders found Egypt virtually undefended by the nominal sovereign power, Christian Byzantium, and they occupied the entire country in less than three years.

The message of Islam was 'There is no God but Allah and Muhammad is his prophet.' Coming from the Arabian peninsular, the invaders spoke Arabic, and soon Arabic became the lingua franca of Egypt, while Greek and Coptic were gradually abandoned as spoken languages. Islam is a religion 'of the book', as distinct from some religions such as Zoroastrianism and animistic cults. It respected both Judaism and Christianity as valid beliefs, albeit inferior to Islam. The Arab armies founded the city of Fustat, on the banks of the Nile at the point where the Nile spreads out into the delta, and this city grew in size to rival the old Greek urban centre of Alexandria. The successive rise and

189

fall of Muslim dynasties is not the subject of this chapter, but suffice it to say that Fustat, renamed Cairo by one twelfth-century North African dynasty, the Fatimids, expanded and became the focal point of the country's political and religious affairs. It was the Fatimids who founded the Al-Azhar University, together with a library and mosques, and until the Ottoman invasion of 1517, the Al-Azhar University was the greatest Muslim seat of learning in the world.

After the Ottoman invasion Cairo was relegated to the status of a provincial city, ruled directly from Constantinople, and it became something of a cultural backwater, cut off from outside influences. For nearly three centuries life there was regulated according to Islamic law, the Sharia, which is a combination of Koranic pronouncements and legal exegesis expanding points where the Koran is unclear or vague. The product of this system was an in-turned and parochial society, but a stable one, confident in the belief that it could withstand any attack from outside, either phsyical or cultural.

Napoleon's invasion in 1799 shattered this belief and demonstrated that an Islamic society, as constituted in Egypt at least, was incapable of repelling attack from a Christian power. And although Muhammad Ali went some way to remedying this weakness after Napoleon's withdrawal, he was only able to do this with the help of another Christian power, Britain. As we have seen in another chapter, the irony of Muhammad Ali's position lay in the fact that his only means of building up a strong army, capable of defending Egypt against the European powers, was to import advisers and technicians from those very countries from which the army was intended to protect her. In the short term, the European powers turned their attention to the crumbling Ottoman Empire in Europe (Greece, Bulgaria, etc.). However, the longer-term cultural threat from Europe to traditional Islamic society was only just beginning. Religious movements in Egypt in the last hundred years have, very broadly speaking, been fighting a prolonged rearguard action against the encroachment of Western European culture.

The nineteenth century as a whole was a period of great intellectual ferment in Egypt, fuelled by the new educated urban élite who had been trained by Europeans and exposed to European ideas and scientific inventions. It was only after 1882, with invasion and subsequent occupation by the British, that Egyptians in general began to feel the need for a definite Islamic response to Europe and its cultural and moral values.

The initial reaction was the formation of a Conservative Reform Movement, led by Sheikh Muhammed Abduh, who later became a very influential Muslim cleric. He and his followers believed that the only way for Islam to confront Western thought and attitudes was to formulate its own characteristic Islamic response to the new ideas and inventions. Only thus would Islamic society be strengthened. The obvious danger inherent in this approach was that acceptance of new ideas and attitudes might well lead to a total rejection of Islam. The Reform Movement found its expression in an organisation calling itself Salaffiyya, which grew up alongside the new emerging secular liberal political parties. By the first decade of the twentieth century, these parties were advocating an Egyptian nationalist response to Europe, and to Britain in particular.

The constitutional arrangements established by Britain in 1923, creating a framework within which the new parties should operate, incidentally struck a blow at the Muslim clerical hierarchy, centred on the Al-Azhar University, and seriously undermined its legitimacy as a major political force in the country. During the three-cornered struggle between the King, the British and the Wafd, the Sheikhs of Al-Azhar, as a rule, supported the King. This was *faute de mieux*, since on the one hand they could in no way benefit from supporting the British, who were responsible for the erosion of their authority in the first place, and on the other hand the Wafd was itself making a bid to steal the popular appeal of traditional Islam.

The patent failure of the Islamic reform movements like Salaffiyya to withstand liberal secular erosion of Islamic traditional beliefs and institutions, produced an inevitable radical Muslim counter-reaction. It started in 1928, when Sheikh Hassan al-Banna formed a militant extremist religio-political movement called the Ihwan al-Muslimin, the Muslim Brotherhood. It offered itself as an alternative to the whole imported European secular political package, and was far more violent in its methods of operation than any of its political contemporaries. Its approach was above all positive. Hassan al-Banna told his followers: 'You are a new soul in the heart of the nation, to give life by means of the Koran.' For true Muslims, he argued, Islam was a complete social and administrative system in itself and already contained all the necessary ingredients of good government.' By returning to a pure version of Islam, and by eliminating the destructive Western influence on a just Islamic society, that society could regenerate itself and regain its pre-eminent position as a dominant world civilisation, as it had been in the Golden Age of Islam, when Europe was still languishing in the early Middle Ages. He strongly contested the suggestion of the Islamic Conservative Reformists that Islamic society could be strengthened through reform. The Brotherhood believed in a fundamental Islamic revival. They demanded reform of the whole of society as a prelude to the strengthening of Islam, and called for a 'jihad', total war, as the only means of countering external and internal corruption. This philosophy proved to be an inspiration to followers from all social classes, from the peasants to the middle-class urban élite.

The Muslim Brotherhood denounced the whole parliamentary system as a foreign and alien growth. Since the British, not unexpectedly, excluded it from participating in government, it was thereby driven further along the path to violent unconstitutional action. During the 1930s it became clear that the religious reform movements were an ineffectual response to the perceived attacks on Islam. All over Europe, violence was becoming a respectable political weapon, and the Muslim Brotherhood felt encouraged to use violence as a means of capitalising on the patent failure of liberalism to cope with the country's economic and social problems. Gradually, the Muslim Brothers established a cell-network and carried out an increasing number of attacks against British property and Army personnel. They used every source of national or religious unrest to stir up their supporters. The Arab rebellion in Palestine in 1936 for the first time gave an anti-Jewish focus to Islamic fervour. During the period of political instability following the Second World War, and inflamed by the Israeli Declaration of Independence in 1948, the Brotherhood stepped up its attacks on British and Jewish property. As the full impact of the Egyptian defeat in the Palestine War sank in, Brotherhood propaganda played on the failure of the parliamentary government to prevent the establishment of the Jewish state. Separate Muslim Brotherhood units fought alongside regular Egyptian Army units, and the defeat and subsequent withdrawal from Palestine was blamed on the King and the decadent liberal Government that had failed to stand up to the Zionists. In 1948, Prime Minister Nuqrashi was assassinated by the Brotherhood; subsequently the Government itself felt obliged to descend to the same level of violence and assassinated Hassan al-Banna, the Supreme Guide of the Brotherhood.

The Brotherhood initially welcomed the Free Officers' revolutionary coup in 1952. However, as it became clear that the Revolutionary Command Council was intent on simply usurping power without sharing it with other groups, the Brotherhood then tried every method possible to embarrass the RCC. It even pressed for an immediate return to constitutional government. The RCC could not cope simultaneously with the double threat from the old political parties and from the Muslim Brotherhood. First it neutralised the political parties, through a combination of repression and the creation of the National Liberation Rally, while the Brotherhood was still left free to criticise. But in 1954, once the parliamentarians had been silenced, the RCC turned on the Brotherhood. The *casus belli* was the attempt by a Muslim Brother to assassinate Nasser on 26 October 1954. A savage campaign ensued of trials, repression and executions, thus securing Nasser his position of unopposed supreme ruler by 1956.

The Free Officers did not wish to eliminate Islam as a popular force. Rather they sought to harness it and use it to bolster up their régime. So, in 1954, with this end in view, and at the very time it was repressing the Brotherhood as a political force, the RCC established an Islamic Congress, of which Anwar Sadat became the Secretary-General. The intention was to fuse the identity of the state with that of Islam and squeeze out any alternative centre of power. In the same year Nasser made the Hadj pilgrimage to Mecca. All this was to demonstrate that the RCC and Nasser were good Muslims and that the country did not need the Muslim Brotherhood to defend Islam. In the heyday of Nasser's rule the Brotherhood kept a low profile. All the while Nasser was being defiant towards the West, as he was over Suez, and making successful approaches to the Soviet bloc, the Brotherhood stood to gain very little by opposing him. It was only when events moved against Nasser that there came a resurgence of fundamentalist Islam.

First there was the prolonged and bloody war in Yemen, which dragged on from 1961 until after the 1967 June War with Israel. This started to sap Nasser's prestige, and every blow to Nasser's authority was an injection of strength to the Muslim Brotherhood. The catastrophe of 1967 produced two circumstances which immediately favoured the Brotherhood: first, with the eclipse, if only temporary, of Nasser's

194

credibility, the extremist religious groups moved in to fill the emotional vacuum with their vision of an alternative society, one that would be strong enough to destroy Israel – or at least force her to give up the Egyptian territory she was occupying. Secondly, Nasser, for his part, was obliged to fall back on Islamic slogans in an effort to re-establish his authority and explain away the June defeat. 'Allah was trying to teach Egypt a lesson,' he said, 'in order to purify her and build a new society.'

The decade of Sadat's rule (1971–81) was a period of growing outrage and fury on the part of the fundamentalists, and especially the Muslim Brotherhood. Until 1973 and the October War it had been muted in its criticism, preferring to bide its time and wait, like all Egyptians, for Sadat to reveal his true colours. Between the time when Sadat consolidated his power in 1971 and the October War of 1973 Sadat, for his part, kept a low profile. It was an uneventful period on the home front, and he was waiting until he would deal that blow to the military and political status quo in the Middle East which would make him a hero and legitimate leader in his own right, and not just the successor to Nasser. Yet, perversely, it was after the October War of 1973 that relations between him and the Brotherhood, and also other extremist groups, began to deteriorate. The reason lies partly in their distrust of Sadat's intentions, and partly in the pressure of outside events.

For one thing, Sadat did not permit the Brotherhood to form a political party, but he did cultivate their support to a certain extent in the hope that they might act as a counterweight to his critics on the left wing. But the Brotherhood used the limited freedom accorded to them to recruit new members from the universities and even from the ranks of the Army. At the same time pressure from Saudi Arabia compelled Sadat to impose at least a semblance of Islamic orthodoxy on Egypt. Saudi Arabia and the Gulf States had both benefited from the massive increase in the

195

world price of oil, and one result of this was that Saudi Arabia had become a major source of aid to Egypt. In return she demanded that religious movements, even of the extreme variety, be tolerated, if not positively encouraged.

Among the rash of smaller fundamentalist groups that appeared in the aftermath of the October War, one notable example was under the leadership of Ahmed Mustafa, and it called itself Takfir wa'l-Hijra (Atonement and Migration). The atonement was for having erred from the true path and the migration (spiritual) was away from present-day society until such time as it had been reformed in accordance with Sharia. This was the group behind Sadat's assassination in 1981. It had been gathering strength since 1973.

Meanwhile, most of the Egyptian people were not eager to lose the benefit of some of the most liberal social laws in the Arab World, so they did not press for action. This seemed to suit Sadat. Whereas Nasser had tried to fuse religion and the state into one object of worship and veneration, Sadat deliberately tried to do the opposite, and separate the two. He declared, in 1979: 'Those who wish to practise Islam can go to the mosques, and those who wish to engage in politics may do so through legal institutions.' This was a clear repudiation of the Brotherhood and all the other fundamentalist groups, who were forced into covert opposition to the régime, much as they had been in the 1930s under the British.

Sadat's visit to Jerusalem in November 1977 to meet the enemy on his own ground, outraged the Brotherhood. They saw it as an act of treachery, selling-out to the Jews who had stolen Arab land from good Muslims and then settled on it themselves. Against the Jews, and in a different way against Sadat, jihad was the only answer. The food riots in 1977 and 1978 gave the fundamentalists a further chance to capitalise on public unrest and dissatisfaction with the régime. Perhaps Sadat over-reacted when he clamped down on all vocal activists and critics of both left and right. He clearly felt that attacks from all quarters threatened his peace policy towards Israel. And in some ways, after Camp David, he had a freer hand in attacking the Brotherhood; for since the Peace Agreements had isolated Egypt from nearly all Arab states, including Saudi Arabia, he could consider himself in a position to ignore protests from that quarter.

Anwar Sadat was assassinated on 6 October 1981, by Muslim extremists directly inspired by the Takfir Wa'l Hijra movement. We now know that the base for this attack was Assiyut, a large city in Upper Egypt and a traditional hotbed of Islamic fundamentalism. We also know that their hatred of Sadat and his behaviour was played upon by Sadat's arch-rival on the international stage, Libyan leader Mu'ammar Qaddafi, who provided support and finance for the rebels. Immediately after the assassination, Libyan radio invited the 'Egyptian people' to rise in revolt and establish an Islamic republic. A few days later violent rioting broke out in Assiyut. But the Egyptian people did not respond to Qaddafi's call for revolution. The lesson to be learnt from Sadat's assassination would seem to be that while there is some disaffection in the country among extremist Islamic groups, it is not widespread among the population as a whole. Nevertheless, it can constitute a fifth column for outside interference in a moment of crisis. When Hosni Mubarak assumed the presidency very shortly after Sadat's death, he resolutely declared that the assassination would not cause the Government to alter its policies in any way, and he sent the Army in to put down the Assiyut riots.

The continuing problem of Islamic fundamentalism, as inherited by President Mubarak, would seem to have been aggravated by events elsewhere in the Arab World. The success of Ayatollah Khomeini in bringing down the apparently invincible Shah from the throne of Iran in 1979 is a source of inspiration for fundamentalists elsewhere. It could be argued that in Iran the rebels were spurred on by a deep and fervent belief that Allah was on their side in their

197

struggle against a corrupt, American-supported régime, and that the Iranian Muslim clergy felt that if they did not act within three to five years it would be too late and they would be muzzled and emasculated for ever. President Mubarak assuredly does not underestimate the value of relating the Iranian experience to Egypt, especially with regard to his relations with the United States. It remains to be seen whether he will act to prevent the emergence of a conspicuously rich, Western-orientated élite, which, cultivated and flattered by the United States, may come to be regarded as socially and morally offensive to Islamic traditionalists. Such a situation could trigger a violent reaction, which could strike not only against that élite but also against its perceived patron, the President himself.

Egypt is a Muslim country, from top to bottom of her society. Her problem is that religion in other parts of the Arab World is being used to harness extremely reactionary, nationalist social forces. Egypt is more advanced than those other countries. There is no reason why she should not find more sophisticated and moderate answers than her neighbours to the destabilising challenges of the twentieth century; but it will take a wise and firm leadership to steer her between the shoals of indigenous religious fervour and foreign domination.

5

The Economy

In his address to Parliament after being elected President of Egypt in 1981, Hosni Mubarak stated: 'Our success will depend upon our ability to face up to the economic issues.' Never was a truer word spoken by an Egyptian leader. In this chapter we shall look at the broad spectrum of economic problems facing Egypt and her leaders, all of which have their roots further back in this century. The problems which face President Mubarak are the same as those which faced Presidents Nasser and Sadat, but over the years they have become increasingly pressing, so that in the 1980s they may well prove to be crucial to Egypt's political future.

During the first part of the nineteenth century Muhammad Ali's approach was, as we have seen, to concentrate all economic activity in his own hands and accumulate capital to finance modernisation. He invested in the expansion of cotton and grain cultivation, and while his main aim was to provide food for the population, and support for the modernisation of the Army, too much of the yield went to the export market and too little was ploughed back into the economy. Thus, while this expansion was a short-term success, it did not have any appreciable effect on the economy in the long run. In the 1870s came the near-collapse of the economy under Khedive Ismail, the imposition of Anglo–French Dual Control, and the subsequent British occupation in 1882. The crisis was a direct result of

199

Ismail's gross over-borrowing from foreign sources to finance his grandiose 'prestige projects' which the economy was both too small and too fragile to support. There was no collapse of agricultural output which had, on the contrary, been growing steadily during the nineteenth century. Egypt had merely been trying to run before she could walk. So the British Agents and Consuls General, Cromer, Gorst and Kitchener, stepped in to put Egypt's financial house in order as a prelude, so the Egyptians assumed, to political independence. This period has been described in chapter 1. Of these three, Cromer was the driving force behind the rescue operation. From his desk in the British Residency he treated Egypt's national finances in the manner of a receiver putting a bankrupt company back on its feet. The results were an unqualified success. By the First World War, Egypt's financial affairs had been placed on a sound footing and she could boast an impressive growth rate. During the nineteenth century as a whole Egypt's agricultural output had risen twelve-fold, and by 1914 it had doubled again.

The aftermath of the First World War, however, marked a turning point for the Egyptian economy. The 1920s saw the beginning of the struggle against the British by the Wafd. The new urban élite which had emerged during the nineteenth century as a result of European involvement, had by now acquired capital and had invested in land. With their political contemporaries, the parliamentary nationalists, they set about trying to diversify and create an 'Egyptian' industrial base; something Muhammad Ali should have done at least half a century earlier. In 1920, they set up a national investment bank, Bank Misr, which accumulated capital and invested in 'national' enterprises and construction companies, which in turn could manufacture goods that had previously had to be imported from abroad, mainly from Britain. Slowly, Egypt progressed from merely exporting agricultural produce and using the hard currency to import consumer goods, to manufacturing them locally and invest-

200

ing the hard currency in the plant rather than the product. This trend was accelerated by the collapse of world cotton prices during the Great Depression and there was a growing realisation that the economic basis of the country could not continue to be dependent upon the vagaries of international commodity prices. Today, many Third World countries face a similar problem. By 1930, the government had realised that developing local industry would need some tariff protection, and protectionist legislation replaced the existing standard 8 per cent import duty with a range of higher selective taxes. Industrial output rose steadily and substantially throughout the 1930s and was further encouraged during the Second World War, when spending by Allied troops on goods and services reduced unemployment, boosted production and expanded the economy generally. However, the benefits of this boom were not enjoyed by the mass of the population. They could not afford any of the consumer goods anyway. In 1942 there were severe food shortages, mainly because world shipping had been disrupted by the war and imports of grain were insufficient to cover consumption. By and large in the rush to industrialise between 1914 and 1945, output in the agricultural sector had been neglected to the extent that in 1945 output was actually lower, despite a substantial rise in population, than it had been in 1918. For all the efforts at industrialisation earlier in the century, industrial output still only accounted for about 10 per cent of Gross National Product. The neglect of agriculture, moreover, meant that growth had not even kept pace with population increase. The recurrent and fundamental problem of food production cannot be divorced from that of land tenure. In 1952 it was estimated that 6 per cent of landowners owned some 65 per cent of the cultivable land. Since in many cases these were absentee landlords their land was not always cultivated well, some of it was not cultivated at all and there was a huge mass of landless peasantry who possessed nothing

201

and worked seasonally on the land of other peasants who managed to own small plots independently.

When the Free Officers seized power in 1952 they may have lacked an overall political strategy but they did realise two important things: first, that there had to be some redistribution of land and indeed reform of the whole system of land tenure, and second the essential link between agriculture and industry. Because some landlords had fled the country after the revolution, large tracts of land had been left fallow. The RCC redistributed land and imposed limits on the size of land holdings so as to prevent a reversion to the status quo ante. Land reform was one of the policies pursued by the Free Officers which was popular and widely recognised as both necessary and just. From the Free Officers' point of view land reform could be implemented by decree without difficulty and at no risk to their own authority. They could safely capitalise on the good will it generated. They realised that industrialisation had not been rapid enough to compensate for the loss of agricultural output, and the years between the revolution of 1952 and the National Charter of 1962 were a period of heavy investment and rapid growth. Whereas in 1952 industrial output had constituted only 10 per cent of GNP, by 1962 this figure was 20 per cent. Such a balance still placed Egypt firmly in the Third World. By way of comparison the Western European average is nearer 70 per cent.

The entry of the Soviet Union into Egyptian affairs after 1955 prompted a radicalisation of economic policies, which was chiefly expressed in a major programme of nationalisation of foreign companies operating in Egypt and government control of investment and capital formation. At the time of Nasser's National Charter all banks, public services and construction companies were nationalised. The first phase was principally directed at American capital but later the principle was extended to cover Egyptian-owned companies. Under the Charter, only 'national capitalism' was

202

permitted. This radicalisation was further encouraged by Egypt's drawing away from the United States and the West towards the non-aligned, Third World bloc. Many of these countries, such as India and Indonesia, were experiencing their own versions of Egypt's economic problems. Economic difficulties mutliplied, mainly on account of the bureaucracy and inefficiency of the public sector. Also there was a great reluctance on the part of foreign investors, especially Americans, to put their money into a country which was avowedly committed to public ownership, and an unwillingness on the part of Western nations in general to give aid to a country which maintained such close ties with the Soviet Union.

This state of economic stagnation, if not decline, was greatly exacerbated by the defeat in the June War of 1967 and the heavy military expenditure involved in a situation of long-term military confrontation with Israel.

Nasser, then, identified the economic problems more comprehensively than his predecessors, and made courageous moves to tackle the root issues of land reform and vested foreign interests. If he failed in his ambition to make Egypt into a modern socialist state, that is a reflection of the enormity of the problem by Western standards. He did not quite escape the chronic weakness of Egyptian leaders for prestige projects; it was perhaps extravagant to build a giant steelworks and an automobile industry while Egypt still lacked a broad base of light consumer industries, but in the case of the Aswan High Dam, he could justifiably boast that he was opening up a whole new dimension in Egypt's economic potential, and in a way that would benefit every section of the population, town-dweller and farmer, rich and poor alike.

Before we look at the modern period under Sadat and Mubarak, let us look at some of the other factors influencing economic progress in Egypt. The most important by far is the massive growth in population. In 1971 it was estimated to be 44 million. By 1983 it was over 44 million. Such figures have horrific implications for economic planners. If present rates continue the population will be over 60 million by the year 2000. The population explosion came about mainly as a result of declining mortality rates, especially among infants, through improved medical facilities. Some 40 per cent of the present population is under sixteen years old. This increase in the number of young people has produced a surfeit of students at the universities, which turn out thousands of qualified graduates every year who have little chance of finding a job they consider worthy of their qualifications. This may explain some of the disaffection and unrest among students and the recent resort to religion as some kind of consolation. In addition, public services such as water supply and drainage have become increasingly inadequate and there is an acute housing shortage, especially in Cairo, where for a long time families have been living in the tombs of Egyptians luckier than themselves. The obvious answer to this problem is birth control, but this is difficult to implement in rural areas where families are unwilling to forgo children who could work in the fields and support their parents in old age. In practice, however, many of these children migrate to the cities and aggravate the social problems there still further. Egypt is forced to concentrate on the twin economic bases of agriculture and manufacturing since she has few natural resources suitable for primary industries. There are some ores and minerals in the desert and some oil in the Sinai, but the quantities extracted are barely sufficient even to meet present needs and soon even these raw materials may have to be imported. There is almost no grazing land for livestock. The only real hope for future economic development lies in greater food production for the home market, more cash-crop farming and widely diversified secondary industries.

The Nile is today, as it has been since time immemorial, the key to agricultural expansion in Egypt. The two dams at

Aswan have greatly helped in the irrigation of cultivated land and even in attempts to reclaim more land from the desert. The first dam was built by the British above Aswan in 1902; it was heightened in 1912 and again in 1933 to provide increased capacity for the expanding population. The post-war population explosion made it imperative that the cultivable area should be extended still further, so a still larger dam was needed if even the status quo were to be maintained. This second dam was started under the auspices of the Soviet Union in 1958 and finally completed in 1970, the year of Nasser's death. It is known as the 'High Dam' and it created behind it an enormous artificial lake called, naturally, Lake Nasser. The High Dam has vast potential, but even so, on its own, without expanded irrigation and a general modernisation of agriculture further downstream, its waters will not irrigate enough land to feed the projected population by the end of the century.

The Suez Canal, since its nationalisation in 1956, has also become a valuable source of national income. It was deepened in 1966 in order to accommodate the very large oil tankers sailing between the Persian Gulf and Europe, only to be blocked a year later during the June War. It was not re-opened until 1975, two years after the October War, when the Disengagement Agreements with Israel brought about the subsequent withdrawal of Israeli troops from the eastern bank. By 1980 it was earning an annual £65 million in revenues for the Egyptian exchequer.

Sadat found Egypt in a parlous economic state when he came to power in 1970. The Suez Canal was blocked, the economy, largely nationalised, was inefficiently dominated by a sluggish and excessive bureaucracy, foreign investment was minimal and foreign aid scarce. Yet huge sums of money were being spent on new Soviet weapons with which to confront Israel. The working population was about 9.5 million, well under 25 per cent of the total population.

Sadat continued Nasser's policy of trying to keep a balance

between industrial and agricultural development so that neither was pushed ahead at the expense of the other. But he shifted the emphasis away from Nasser's scientific socialism. His preferred solution was to opt for a free market economy which would attract foreign investment while still maintaining some public enterprises which would compete with the private sector. His 1980 Constitution declared that: 'Egypt is a democratic socialist state with a mixed economy.' Sadat called his brand of liberalisation 'infitah', opening up, and it did indeed help to open up Egypt again to foreign investors, especially after the 1973 War. As hopes for a lasting peace rose dramatically after Sadat's visit to Jerusalem in 1977, the economic climate seemed to furnish an unprecedentedly stable environment for attracting investment. Yet, once again, much of the ensuing investment was not in the long-term interests of the country as a whole; rather, it was for a quick profit, for example in tourism, and failed to benefit the bulk of the people thus resulting in very little tangible fixed capital formation. From the foreign investment that remained in Egypt, much of the profit found its way into the hands of a new élite of entrepreneurs who had benefited from infitah, and who were known for their conspicuous consumption and ostentatious life-style which was associated with Sadat's ruling coterie. The gap remained, and even widened between these beneficiaries of infitah and the mass of the population who remained impoverished and unemployed, living in appalling conditions and seeing no hope of bettering their lot under Sadat's régime.

When Mubarak came to power in 1981, he must have been aware of the fact that the main popular grievance against Sadat had been that the long-awaited economic benefits of peace with Israel had not materialised. In fact the economic situation had actually deteriorated since the peace treaty with Israel, because financial assistance from major oil-producing states like Saudi Arabia had been suspended in protest at the treaty. Mubarak's economy strategy was to call for a 'productive open-door policy'. This was to involve somewhat paradoxically building up home industries and if possible increasing foreign investment in those industries, together with curbs on imports. Mubarak is above all a pragmatist. He has not claimed to have a master-plan to offer Egypt or a facile optimism that the economy will pick up on its own. When he came to power, subsidies on essential goods were costing the state £180 million every year; and this simply to keep people off the streets and prevent rioting and looting. The short- and even medium-term economic prospects are indeed bad. Yet Egyptian planners do have some assets: relatively stable governmental institutions, a mature commercial infrastructure, a good road and rail network, an international waterway running through the national territory and several good ports.

Egypt has a large potential labour force, a long-standing commercial middle class and a national sense of common historical identity. What she needs now is the right leader.

Perhaps, in Hosni Mubarak, Egypt has at last produced a President who does realise the crucial importance of economic issues and their intimate connection with the political stability of the country. He is by report a pragmatist who sees his role, not just as a political figure-head but also as a manager and administrator of the nation's affairs.

6

Foreign Policy

In this chapter we shall confine ourselves, for the most part, to Egypt's foreign relations after the final break with Britain in 1956, because only after that did Egypt assume real control of her relations with other countries. We shall look first at relations with the Soviet Union, then with the United States, after that with other Arab states and Israel. As for Egypt's relations with Europe, from the end of the Second World War to 1955, these had been virtually confined to Britain. Britain's retreat from Empire under the post-war Labour Government was part of a general reassessment of her foreign relations. The political will simply no longer existed to maintain her overseas commitments. As early as 1948 she had abandoned Palestine to partition, and a year later left India on the verge of civil war. The founding of the United Nations Organisation in 1945 meant that this body usurped some of Britain's functions as international policeman and arbitrator. Egypt was a founder member of the UN, and immediately took her case against Britain to this new international forum. Now Britain was no longer in a position to stifle the complaints of her erstwhile protectorate, as she had done in 1919 when Saad Zaglul had tried unsuccessfully to plead his country's case at the Versailles peace conference. After the Suez crisis, which has been dealt with in earlier chapters, neither Britain nor Egypt was inclined to renew relations. Later Britain applauded Sadat's peace initiative with Israel, deplored his assassination, observed his successor with interest, but by and large she has preferred to remain an uninvolved spectator.

Egypt, for her part, had gradually realised during the 1950s that while Britain had been the European victor in 1945, in reality it was American and Soviet military strength which had tipped the scales against the Axis powers. It became clear that Britain would in future play a declining role in world politics. The immediate post-war domination of most of Europe by American and Soviet forces led to military and ideological competition, and this soon spread to other areas of the world. The Cold War was under way.

Cold War competition did not affect Egypt until 1955, by which time Nasser had become the undisputed ruler and was beginning to look beyond Egypt's frontiers. In 1955 he emerged on to the world stage and struck up friendship with, amongst others, President Tito of Yugoslavia and Pandit Nehru of India. In April of that same year, a conference of Non-Aligned Nations was held in Bandung. There, Nasser succeeded in establishing himself as the Arab spokesman of the non-aligned group of countries who did not wish to become embroiled in the superpower struggle and therefore refused to take sides with either the Soviet Union or the United States. In this new international capacity he put himself, in the eyes of the world, on the same footing as Zhou Enlai of communist China and Sukarno of Indonesia. It was, on the face of it, a sound move from his point of view. It conferred on both Egypt and Nasser an independent national identity and international prestige. If his new-found role as Arab spokesman for the non-aligned bloc obliged him to distance himself from the West, and especially from the United States and Britain, that in no way conflicted with his personal inclinations.

Egypt and The Soviet Union

It took the Soviet Union nearly a decade to recover from the ravages of the Second World War. During that time her foreign policy goals were very simple: to consolidate her position in Eastern Europe, to achieve military parity with the United States, and in pursuance of this goal, to assert her influence in the Middle East as Britain's authority there declined. Her first positive step into the area was the Czech Arms Deal of 1955. Egypt needed arms because she was genuinely afraid of Israel's military build-up, but she was excluded from British or American arms supplies as a reprisal for refusing to contemplate joining the Western-sponsored Bagdad Pact. Therefore she looked eastwards. In view of the Cold War the Soviet Union was loath to supply arms publicly and so the deal was arranged through her ally, Czechoslovakia. By 1956 Egypt had acquired about 150 Russian-built planes and 300 tanks; however, these had no real impact on the outcome of the 1956 war, although the Soviet Union did rhetorically threaten both London and Paris with rocket attacks if they did not comply with the American-sponsored UN resolution that they should withdraw. After the war the arms continued to flow. If Nasser occasionally found Russian diplomacy a little heavy-handed he compared it not unfavourably to his past experience with Britain and the United States. In any case once he had accepted their patronage he had no choice but to continue the relationship. Britain and the United States, either incensed or worried at his behaviour, withdrew their offer of financial aid for the High Dam at Aswan. The Soviet Union was only too pleased to step in and save Egypt from humiliation. Soviet influence increased generally over the next decade; military aid was bolstered by economic assistance, Russian technicians built the High Dam, even though Nasser boasted of it as a spectacular Egyptian achievement.

After a while Nasser became almost as irritated at Russian heavy-handedness as he had been in the past with British arrogance, and even went so far as to compare the Soviet Ambassador to the once-detested British High Commissioner.

For all Nasser's adoption of Soviet-style 'scientific socialism' and the National Charter of 1962, he was never convinced by doctrinaire communism, finding it alien to an Arab society and atheist in the context of Islam.

It is now generally acknowledged that the catastrophe of the June War stemmed indirectly from action by the Soviet Union. The Soviet leadership informed Nasser that Israel was massing for an attack on all fronts. Nasser believed this, and prepared to launch a pre-emptive strike. Israel took this action as a *casus belli* and on the morning of 5 June Israeli war-planes destroyed over two-thirds of the Egyptian airforce while it was still on the ground. This was a combined humiliation for Egypt and the Soviet Union. They had not only seemingly been misinformed, but it was largely Soviet arms which were destroyed or captured by the Israelis. Nasser never recovered from the shock of this defeat. He died three years later a broken man, leaving behind him a country economically stultified and heavily reliant on Soviet support and aid.

Sadat's over-riding aim, when he came to power, was to wipe away the defeat of 1967. His first priority was to force or persuade Israel to withdraw from the Sinai peninsula. In order to achieve this, he had to convince at least Israel, and both the superpowers, that there could be no Middle East settlement of any sort until this minimal demand had been satisfied. Sadat allowed the Soviet Union to continue to build up Egypt's advanced weaponry, especially along the Suez Canal until by 1972 he felt that the Egyptian army could wage a successful war against Israel without Russian backing. At this point he expelled nearly 15,000 Soviet military advisers. In Washington and Tel Aviv the generals rejoiced.

Sadat's real motive was to ensure that the next war would be a truly Egyptian victory. And so it was – almost. Only in the closing days of the war, when the Egyptian Third Army found itself surrounded in the Sinai Desert, did the Soviet Union go so far as to mobilise airborne troops ready to be sent to the battle zone in Egypt's defence. However when U.S. President Richard Nixon placed American forces world-wide on nuclear alert, this brought about a cessation of hostilities without delay.

The ensuing Geneva Conference and the American-sponsored disengagement agreement between Egypt and Israel did nothing to stem the steady decline of Soviet influence in Egypt and in the Middle East as a whole.

Egypt and the United States

The United States had been virtually excluded from Egyptian affairs until after the October War of 1973. Sadat opened the door to them when he expelled the Soviet advisers in 1972, and his policy of infitah invited American investment and eventually aid, at first economic and later military. Despite the Egyptian 'victory' of the October War, it had in fact left Egypt with less territory than before. Israeli forces were firmly entrenched on both sides of the Suez Canal, and Sadat realised that it was only the United States who could contain Israel in the long run. He also perceived that in the last resort America would never allow Israel to be defeated on the battlefield. 'The U.S.' he remarked, 'holds 99 per cent of the cards in this game.'

Sadat was only too pleased to go along with Kissinger's shuttle diplomacy after 1973, and this paid dividends in that it led to the first Egyptian-Israeli disengagement agreement in 1974, under which Israeli troops withdrew from the West bank of the Canal. After this proof of American goodwill and ability to influence Israel, he restored diplomatic relations with Washington which had been broken off since 1967. In 1975 a second disengagement agreement secured a further Israeli withdrawal from the east bank of the Canal and the return to Egypt of the Abu Rodeis oil-fields on the western edge of the Sinai Desert. Sadat saw everything to be gained from courting the United States. By this time America was pumping generous amounts of aid, both military and economic, into Egypt; the unspoken condition of this being that Sadat should keep his relations with the Soviet Union at a low level.

Sadat did not make his historic journey to Jerusalem in November 1977 because he was dissatisfied with the course of events under American auspices, but rather in response to internal pressures. In January of that year there had been serious food riots in both Cairo and Alexandria, and Sadat felt that his whole economic policy was under attack. He saw a need to bolster his personal prestige as a national leader. The message he took to Jerusalem was peace in the Middle East, but he was well aware that by taking his case into the enemy's camp he was making himself a target for hostility from the rest of the Arab World. He was, in effect, placing Egypt even more firmly in the hands of America. Washington gave her unreserved blessing to Sadat's initiative and was only too pleased to step in and preside over the ensuing negotiations at Camp David. She now had two client states in the Middle East. As guarantor of the peace treaty which was signed between Israel and Egypt in March 1979, she had now consolidated her hold over the region.

The new Israeli-Egyptian axis became the backbone of American military strategy in the area, and this was seen as a counterbalance to the Soviet-orientated alliance between Syria and Libya. American and Egyptian forces now hold regular military manoeuvres, but the relationship has not yet progressed to the point where Israeli and Egyptian forces take part in joint operations.

The assassination of Sadat in October 1981 thoroughly

alarmed the United States, who feared that their strategy might be about to collapse and that they had been unwise to allow it to rest so heavily on one man. They were greatly relieved to find that the new President, Hosni Mubarak, committed himself from the outset to continuing the foreign policies of his predecessor. Moreover, as time passed, it became clear that Mubarak had the solid backing of the Egyptian establishment. There was never any question of Egypt abandoning either her relationship with the United States or the peace treaty with Israel.

Egypt, the Arab World and Israel

Nasser had two broad foreign policy aims, one was Arab Unity and the other the destruction of Israel.

In order to understand many aspects of Egypt's relations with the Arab World, one has to bear in mind the amorphous concepts of Arab Nationalism and Arab Unity. Arab Nationalism is the belief that all Arabs are one nation, bound together by a common religion, a common language, a common heritage and a common destiny. The Arab Nation transcends individual national boundaries, which are seen as the product of past European colonialism. Arab Unity is simply the ideal of eliminating all these artificial, imposed borders. The first natural objective of Arab Nationalism was to eradicate the influence of the erstwhile colonial powers throughout the Arab World. The second was to unite the Arab states by any available means.

In Egypt the Wafd were the nationalists who finally ejected the British, while Nasser strove to achieve unity with any willing Arab state. His first attempt was the creation of the UAR in 1958 when the Syrian Ba'ath nationalists opted for political union with Egypt. One can only understand why the Syrians were prepared to surrender their independence in this way if one looks at it in the light of the nebulous

214

concept of Arab Unity. It was only after three years that the Syrians realised that Nasser's idea of Arab Unity involved total submission to a single government, in this case Egypt. At this point Syria seceded from the Union amidst recriminations and disillusionment. The Syrian episode cast some doubts on the feasibility or even the desirability of physical union between Arab states, although this continues to be the declared aim of many Arab régimes.

Having tried unsuccessfully to involve Egypt in pan-Arab affairs, Nasser turned his attention to the safety of domestic issues. Although he committed Egyptian troops to the war in Yemen from 1961 to 1967, this was merely a military adventure; the only outcome of it was to weaken the army at home and severely strain relations with Saudi Arabia. It had no diplomatic purpose and resulted in no tangible benefit to Egypt.

Apart from the desirability of Arab Unity *per se*, it was perceived as an essential preliminary to the military defeat of Israel. When the Joint Arab armies invaded Palestine in 1948, they did so because they instinctively felt that they could not allow the implantation of an alien Zionist state in Arab territory. But by 1967 Nasser could rally both Syrian and Jordanian military support under the banner of Arab Unity. The ensuing Israeli victory was therefore seen as a collective defeat of the Arab Nation as a whole and not just a military defeat of the three countries actively involved in the fighting. Throughout his presidency Nasser's relations with Israel were wholly military and have already been dealt with in the chapter on the Army. The limited success of the October War of 1973 was made possible by co-operation between Egypt and Syria in the initial attack; it showed that a combination of Arab countries was capable of organising and implementing a joint strategy. Had this been the case in 1948, Israel would probably not have survived.

Political wrangling between Arab leaders tends to be misunderstood by outsiders. One day they threaten each

215

other with war and the next embrace each other as sworn brothers. The fact is, that despite political differences they feel they share a common bond of being Arab. This leaves them free to quarrel openly like brothers, but by that same token means that reconciliation can be swift and without lasting rancour. Hand in hand with this sense of kinship comes a nebulous idea of a common Arab interest *vis à vis* the rest of the world. This was never so evident as when Sadat stepped outside the circle and journeyed to Jerusalem. The other Arab states mustered a greater measure of unity against the traitor Sadat than they ever had against the arch-enemy Israel.

Conclusion

Both Egypt and Israel are at important junctures in their respective development. Peace has brought to each the chance to take stock and choose their priorities for the years ahead; a privilege they have both hitherto been denied, living as they have under the shadow of war. What have they made of peace?

On both sides the story is one of missed opportunity. Israel has suffered from a surfeit of unemployed generals, one or two of whom have given the international media the spectacle of Fortress Israel at its most chauvinistic. They have seen peace with Egypt as an invitation to unleash an open-ended war on the northern frontier. Even when the Kahane Commission of Enquiry created the illusion that the Knesset could still rein in the military, the Cabinet lacked the political will to carry out its forthright recommendations.

In Egypt, on the other hand, the President positively relies on the Army in order to remain in power. This is not to say that he is not the legitimately elected President, but in the last resort it is the Army and not Parliament that can remove him from power. Unlike Israel, Egypt does not have a standing army, and the High Command constitutes a permanent rival centre of power to the presidency.

The politicians in Israel, far from using peace as a golden opportunity to put some order into the fundamentally unsound economy, have felt free to dig up the hatchet of

217

personal rivalries. Old divisions have widened between right and left, Ashkenazi and Sephardi, secular and religious. In Egypt, in a very different political environment, Hosni Mubarak must not pass up the opportunity to experiment with genuine multi-party government; though in all fairness he may well feel the top priority for the next few years should be to guarantee social stability in the country. He cannot fail to have learnt from Sadat's experience of parliamentary parties, some of which, once in Parliament, had every interest in seeing the system collapse.

The general public in Israel has felt that after peace with Egypt the time has come for loosening belts and reaping some of the rewards of thirty years of restraint. They went on a spending spree, aided and abetted by a feckless Treasury Department. Peace has allowed Israel to choose what she will do with the Occupied Territories and has opened a schism between religious and non-religious Jews, who tend to have conflicting ideas on the subject. All the while Israel was at war there was no question of withdrawing from the West Bank or the Gaza Strip, for strategic reasons. Now, continued occupation has to be legitimised on religious grounds. This has not been the only factor in the disquieting resurgence of religious fervour. A lot of noise is made by a small vocal minority which is unlikely ever to be a threat to the stability of the state. In Egypt, on the other hand, the religious fervour of the Muslim extremists already threatens to permeate all sections of society, and, left unchecked, could quickly undermine the whole fabric of Egyptian society.

This is where the big difference lies, and what makes Egypt the more unstable partner in peace, since peace has brought no tangible benefits to the mass of the people. Israel has problems, but there most people are better off and feel genuinely and fundamentally more secure since the peace with Egypt.

A Select Bibliography

Israel

ALLON Yigal: *The Making Of Israel's Army* London 1970

BALL George: 'US-Israeli Relations' *Foreign Affairs*, 1979

BAR-ZOHAR Michel: *The Armed Prophet* (Ben Gurion) London 1967

BEGIN Menachem: *The Revolt: Story of the Irgun* New York 1951

BRECHER: *The Foreign Policy System of Israel* Oxford 1972

BRECHER: *Decisions in Israel's Foreign Policy* Oxford 1972

CURTIS Michael (and Susan GITTELS): *Israel and the Third World* New Jersey 1976

DAYAN Moshe: *Story of My Life* London 1976

EBAN Abba: *An Autobiography* London 1978

EISENSTADT S. N.: *Israeli Society* London 1968

FRANKEL William: *Israel Observed* London 1980

HOROWITZ David: *The Economics of Israel* London 1967

KRAMMER: *The Forgotten Friendship* (with the USSR) Illinois 1974

MEIR Golda: *My Life* London 1976

PERES Shimon: *David's Sling* New York 1970

PERES Shimon: *From All These Men* London 1979

PERLMUTTER Amos: *Politics and the Military in Israel 1967–77* London 1978

PRITTIE Terence: *Eshkol of Israel* London 1969

RABIN Yitzhak: *The Rabin Memoirs* London 1979

SAFFRAN Nadau: *The Embattled Ally* London 1973

ST JOHN Robert: *Eban* London 1972

SCHLAIM and YANIV: 'Domestic Politics and Foreign Policy in Israel' *International Affairs* Spring 1980

SMART Ian: 'Oil, the Superpowers and the Middle East' *International Affairs* 1977

SACHAR Howard M.: *A History of Israel* Oxford 1977

WEIZMANN Chaim: *Trial and Error* New York 1949

BE'ERI Eliezer: *Army Officers in Arab Politics and Society*
New York 1970
BERGUE Jacques: *Egypt: Imperialism and Revolution*
London 1972
CROMER Lord: *Modern Egypt* London 1908
DODWELL Henry: *The Founder of Modern Egypt*
Cambridge 1967
GIBB H. A. R.: *Modern Trends in Islam* Chicago 1947
HEIKAL M.: *The Road to Ramadan* London 1975
HEIKAL M.: *Nasser, the Cairo Documents* London 1972
HEIKAL M.: *The Sphinx and the Commissar* London 1978
HIRST D. and BEESON I.: *Sadat* London 1981
HOPWOOD D.: *Egypt: Politics and Society 1945–1981*
London 1982
HOURANI Albert: *Arabic Thought in the Liberal Age*
London 1962
ISSAWI Charles: *Egypt in Revolution* London 1963
KERR M.: *The Arab Cold War 1958–64* Oxford 1965
LOVE K.: *Suez: the Twice Fought War* London 1969
MITCHELL R.: *The Society of Muslim Brothers* Oxford
1969
SADAT Anwar el-: *In search of identity* London 1977
SADAT Anwar el-: *Revolt on the Nile* London 1957
STEPHENS R.: *Nasser: a Political Biography* London 1971
VATIKIOTIS P. J.: *Nasser and his Generation* London 1978
VATIKIOTIS P. J.: *The History of Egypt from Muhammad
Ali to Sadat* London 1976
VATIKIOTIS P. J.: *The Egyptian Army in Politics*
Greenwich, Conn. 1975

Index

221

222

223

Mapam 34
Maronite Christians 58, 59, 61
Mecca 194
Med-Dead Canal 89
Meir, Golda 27, 30, 41, 58, 64, 100
Middle East Defence Pact 106
Millet System 20, 71
Misr al-Fatat *see* Young Egypt
Mizrachi party 73
Mizrachi Workers party 73
Mobutu 122
Morocco 43, 107, 111, 121
Moshav 18, 34, 64, 80
Mubarak, President Hosni 164, 165,
    186, 187, 188, 197, 198, 199, 203,
    206, 207, 214
Muhammad Ali 145, 159, 168, 190, 199,
    200
Muheiddin, Khalid 162
Munich Games 117
Muslim Brotherhood 116, 147, 151, 152,
    159, 164, 173, 175, 176, 183, 192,
    193, 194, 195, 196, 197

Nahas, Mustafa 150, 155, 172
Napoleon, Emperor 168, 190
Nasser, Gamal 55, 56, 57, 93, 97, 99,
    106, 107, 113, 114, 117, 145, 148,
    149, 150, 151, 152, 153, 154, 155, 156,
    157, 158, 159, 160, 161, 162, 163,
    164, 165, 172, 173, 175, 177, 178, 179,
    180, 181, 182, 194, 195, 196, 199,
    202, 203, 205, 206, 209, 210, 211, 214,
    215
National Assembly, Egypt 156, 157,
    161, 162, 163, 183, 187
National Assembly, Israel 36
National Charter 156, 157, 202, 211
National Democratic party 163
NPUO (National Progressive Union
    Organisation) 162
NPUP (National Progressive Union
    Party) 162, 163
NRP (National Religious Party) 73, 74,
    75, 76, 77
National Union 152
NATO 111
Navon, President Yitzhak 37
Nazareth 87
Negev 19, 42, 82, 84, 85, 110, 149
Neguib, Muhammed 150, 151, 160

Nehru, Jawaharlal 97, 120, 175, 209
New Economic Policy 82, 99
Nigeria 120
Nile 189, 204
Nixon, Richard 212
Non-Aligned Nations, 175, 209
nuclear programme in Israel 88, 109
Nuqrashi, Mahmud 193

OAU (Organisation for African Unity)
    121
October Paper 161
October War 58, 61, 66, 101, 114, 121,
    161, 165, 185, 195, 205, 211–2, 215
Occupied Territories 32, 33, 44, 57, 76,
    80, 86, 104, 114, 115, 121, 122
oil 22, 24, 56, 61, 80, 85, 96, 100, 101,
    121, 196
Operation Litani 61
Operation Musketeer 107, 108, 109
Operation Peace for Galilee 48, 49, 62,
    104, 118, 123
OPEC 100, 101
Orabist Revolt 132–3, 169–70
Oriental Jews 43, 46, 50, 69, 75, 76, 83,
    86, 87

Pakistan 119
Palestine War 149, 193 *see also*
    Independence
Palmach 30, 32, 41, 44, 53, 64, 65
Paris 56, 107
Passfield White Paper 19
'Peace Now' movement 49
Peres, Shimon 34, 41, 42, 44, 45, 51,
    54, 55, 67, 68, 77, 79, 87, 99, 102,
    106, 107
petrochemicals industry, Israel 85
Phalangists 50, 59, 62, 77
PLO (Palestine Liberation Organisation)
    62, 63, 104, 112, 113, 114, 118, 121,
    122, 123
Poalei Zion 17, 80
Provisional Council of Israel 27, 72

Qaddafi 197
Quatly, Shikri 155

Rabin, Yitzhak 32, 44, 45, 64, 65, 66,
    67, 100
rabbinate 21

225

United States 26, 31, 48, 56, 61, 62, 63, 79, 92, 94, 95, 96, 97, 98, 99, 100, 101, 102, 103, 104, 105, 108, 110, 111, 119, 122, 160, 164, 176, 177, 178, 181, 183, 184, 185, 198, 203, 208, 209, 210, 211, 212, 213, 214
UNSCOP Report 26, 28, 29, 33

Va'ad Leumi 35
Venice Declaration 112, 113
Versailles Peace Conference 16, 17, 135, 208

Wafd 148, 150, 155, 172, 191, 200, 214
War of Attrition 57, 100, 182
Water Carrier (Israel) 84–5, 88, 89
Weizmann, Chaim 14, 15, 25, 34, 35
Weizmann, Ezer 67
West Bank *see* Occupied Territories
Wingate, Orde 22, 64, 67
Workers Federation *see* Histadrut

World War 1914–18 *see* First World War
World War 1939–45 *see* Second World War
World Zionist Organisation 34

Yadin, Yigal 67
Yemen 43, 46, 83, 97, 156, 157, 179, 215
Yom Kippur *see* October War
'Young Egypt' 147
Yugoslavia 209

Zaglul, Saad 208
Zaire 120, 122
Zhou Enlai 209
Zim 120
Zionism 13, 14, 17, 20, 69, 70, 71, 80, 94, 96, 98, 120
Zionist Congress 27
Zionist Workers Front *see* Poalei Zion
Zoroastrianism 189